FAST-TRACK
CAREERS FOR THE
90s

FAST-TRACK
CAREERS FOR THE
90s

Adele Lewis
Doris Kuller

SCOTT, FORESMAN AND COMPANY
Glenview, Illinois   London

ACKNOWLEDGMENT

I wish to acknowledge Joal Hetherington as a coauthor of this book and to extend appreciation for her invaluable contribution as copyeditor and typist of the manuscript.

Doris Kuller

Material found on pages 52–57 previously published in RN, the full-service nursing journal. Copyright © 1988 Medical Economics Company, Inc., Ordell, N.J. Reprinted by permission.

Library of Congress Cataloging-in-Publication Data

Lewis, Adele Beatrice
    Fast-track careers for the 90s / Adele Lewis, Doris Kuller.
      p.   cm.
    1. Vocational guidance. 2. Occupations. 3. Professions.
    I. Kuller, Doris.   II. Title.
    HF5381.L357   1989
    331.7′02—dc20

1 2 3 4 5 6 MPC 94 93 92 91 90 89

ISBN 0-6733-38075-0

Scott, Foresman professional books are available for bulk sales at quantity discounts. For information, please contact Marketing Manager, Professional Books Group, Scott, Foresman and Company, 1900 East Lake Avenue, Glenview, IL 60025.

CONTENTS

SECTION THREE

A NEW LOOK AT THE OLD PROFESSIONS

5

6

7

8

9

10

11

SECTION FOUR

DREAM JOBS: ON YOUR OWN

12

13

THE SHIFTING OF AMERICA

Change: the watchword of our times. The foods on our tables change; the items advertised on our televisions are continually replaced by new and altered products; we move from apartment to apartment and house to house. And from job to job to job, sometimes into fields and positions that had never even been dreamed of a couple of decades ago.

That, of course, is one of the most tantalizing riddles facing most of us in the years ahead, on whose solution rests our security and our means to enjoy the fruits of this prolific age. Which jobs will offer opportunities to leap ahead, to capitalize on all of this change; which will languish? To unravel that puzzle, we must grasp the significant changes that are sweeping our society and economy along. We can't take control of what we don't understand.

What are the forces that are shaping our immediate futures? In the coming decade, two factors will irrevocably change the job market: the aging of the massive baby boom generation, and the ongoing transformation of America into a service economy.

1

The Facts of Life

By the 1990s, American society will be dominated by the middle-aged. One-third of the population will be between the ages of 45 and 54. The baby boomers will have moved from young and yuppie to middle-aged and middle-class. Surprising? No—not given the facts.

After the Second World War, the forties and fifties generation felt displaced—uprooted. They were obsessive about picking up the threads of their interrupted lives and avid to stake their claim in America. They wanted homes, cars, job security, stability, and above all they yearned for the assurance of continuity—namely, children. The women who gave birth to the baby boom generation broke the long historical pattern of each generation having fewer children than the preceding one. Instead, they had more children than their mothers did. Essentially, they didn't settle, as their offspring believe, for a settled life. They chose it. The result? A bulging baby boom—a generation, according to the U.S. Census Bureau, some 78 million strong.

But here's the switch: When the baby boomers came of age, they chose not to settle down, not to join the establishment, and not to start families. The majority of the boomers postponed having children until they were well into their thirties. And not only did the baby boomers wait longer to start families, but they are having fewer children than any other generation. Demographers predict that nearly 20 percent of baby boom women will not have children at all. As if by some mysterious consensus, the boomers tipped the population scale. Today, they far outweigh every other population group, particularly the young. This affinity shift has secured the sixties generation's continued influence in shaping the style and priorities of America well into the twenty-first century. By sheer numbers and collective power, they will hold their grip on America's values for a long time. Some predict that their power will last for the next fifty years as their children and grandchildren take on the traditions the baby boom has created.

Given this imbalance, what is the readout for the rest of the population? Perhaps most startling is that for the first time in the United States, there are more people 65 years old and over than people aged 18 and under. Also, there has been a marked drop and continuing decline in the numbers of young adults between the ages of 18 and 24. And by the year 2000, the major population share will be held by people 55 years old and over.

The second most influential factor affecting the population profile, after the baby boomers, is the relatively rapid increase in our life spans as biomedical advances enable the aged to live longer. The real shocker is reported by the renowned medical ethicist Dr. Daniel Callahan in his book *Setting Limits*. He reveals with some alarm that, proportionately, the fastest-growing age group in the United States is the over-85s. Children born in 1987, Callahan points out, can expect to live sixteen years longer on average than their grandparents who were born in 1930. Statisticians envision life spans routinely extending beyond 100. Whether or not you agree with Dr. Callahan that longer is not necessarily better and share his concern about the serious threat this poses to the economics of our health care system, the irrefutable fact is that America is aging.

Aside from being an interesting turnaround, how will this swing of the age pendulum affect which careers will sizzle and which will fizzle in the 1990s?

Cheryl Russell, editor-in-chief of *American Demographics* magazine and author of *100 Predictions for the Baby Boom*, sizes it up this way.

> I believe the nineties will be a good decade, because the most influential group, the middle-aged baby boomers, will hit their peak earning years and therefore will be the most affluent as well. And the way they spend and save that money will change dramatically. Baby boomers will get serious about retirement planning. The growing financial services market will feel the surge as middle-aged parents grapple with the best way to save for retirement and pay college bills.

Russell also predicts that the current baby boomlet will have dwindled by the late nineties; this will trigger a shift in demand from day-care centers and nursery schools to alternative private schools. She maintains that these parents who are used to paying for child care will not be averse to private-sector tuition costs, providing that the public educational system does not improve. Another interesting forecast Russell makes is that the baby boomers will be spending more time at home with their kids—a trend that will help change the national buying and entertainment habits. "VCRs, home gyms, and catalogue and TV shopping will be even more on the upswing as people look toward home-oriented leisure," she observes.

Since the baby boomers comprise the all-time biggest consumer market in history, and since the older and richer they become the stronger their economic clout will be, careers that cater to their needs and indulgences will flourish. *Fortune* magazine compiled a wish-list for this heavyweight generation that covered the gamut from furniture to computers, cars to children's products. *Fortune* wisely included the need for financial services to help boomers finance their debts once they've splurged on their wish-list. As indicated by the *Fortune* piece, American businesses are already trying to figure out what these middle-aged baby-boom consumers will want in order to take advantage of their buying power.

Russel's book relates a telling example of the power of the baby-boom market in the recent Coca-Cola fiasco. The Coca-Cola Company assessed the aging sixties generation and decided they were passé in terms of the soft-drink market. The powers that be concluded that teenagers drink more soft drinks than people in their twenties and thirties, and they went after that younger market. They introduced a sweeter and less fizzy new Coke. (Pepsi also jumped on the teen-wagon, flooding television screens with elaborate videos of Michael Jackson dancing and singing the praises of Pepsi; the campaign probably sold more Michael Jackson records than Pepsis.) What the cola companies overlooked was the giant size of the boomer market, as opposed to the relatively small numbers of the baby bust generation. After Coca-Cola made the switch, it was inundated with complaints; within just three months, it was forced to bring back the old Coke. A year later, Coke Classic was outselling new Coke by four to one. The lesson is clear. Though youth was once the most important market in the country because of the baby boom, older Americans—in other words, that same generation—now control the marketplace.

What kinds of medical, legal, and financial services will they need? What form do their indulgences take? How will their perennial youth-worship affect the boomers' needs as they try to stave off middle age and hold on to their youthful looks? One instance: According to *New York* magazine, plastic surgery is one of the fastest-growing medical specialties in the country. Almost any fast-track career in the 1990s will hinge on knowing these middle-aged baby boomers in order to target the market.

Several significant factors shape the baby boom profile:

First, from all the evidence, the middle-aged baby boomers' priorities, lifestyles, and self-image differ from those of any other recent middle-aged generation. A 1981 Louis Harris study of college-educated baby boomers revealed that most believe their generation is different from other generations living today. It is hard to argue the point, since it would seem that what many of them fought for as teenagers they realized as adults—a society of diversity instead of conformity.

Second, the baby boom group is less provincial, more inclined to be global in tastes, than their parents and grandparents. According to the American Society for Quality Control, in a study conducted by the Gallup Organization in 1985, only 48 percent of baby boomers believe that American-made products are of better quality than imports. Their loyalty, the evidence shows, is to quality. American businesses in the 1990s whose target is the middle-aged boomers will have to convince them that "Made in America" means quality once again.

Perhaps the most significant and enduring characteristic of the boomers is their open attitude to new things and their willingness to experiment with everything from exotic foods and special running shoes to video cameras and personal computers. Given this inherent attraction to the new, they are sure to want and accept new ways of buying things as well. In fact, the signs are already undeniable. Mediamark Research, Inc., reported that in 1984 half of all the baby boomers bought something through the mail. Randall Smith predicted in the *Wall Street Journal* that by the mid-1990s, one-fourth to one-third of all retail sales in the United States will take place out-of-store through such means as television shopping channels, 800 numbers, and mail-order catalogs.

In addition, the boomers' love affair with electronics will remain intense. In an August 1985 issue of *Adweek*, William Meyers noted that the baby boom has transformed television from a passive viewing technology into an active one. In the 1990s, the VCR will be as common as the television. The advertising agency BBD&O foresees that by 1990, only two-thirds of the television audience at any given time will be watching network programs, while the rest of the audience is recording programs with VCRs or viewing rented movies, cable television, or movie channels. As each sophisticated new technology is introduced, the baby boomers will be the first Americans to adopt it—they will have both the money and the inclination.

Another interesting characteristic of the boomers is their need to acquire experience, as well as material objects. James Ogilvy, a researcher for the Stanford Research Institute, says, "The real meaning of the information revolution lies in the growth of the experience industry; not a computer in every home, but an increasingly wide range of experiences." The travel industry pitches experience along with vacation. Digs, safaris, theater tours, art tours, architectural tours, and so on have become a standard part of the travel lure. "New" is the operative word for the baby boom consumer.

Those treading on the heels of the baby boomers will enjoy a wide-open job market as the boomers never did. The continuing drop in the numbers of young adults between the ages of 18 and 24 has resulted in a notable labor shortage for entry-level jobs. Supporting evidence is everywhere. Employment agencies are competing for young, qualified people. Sy Cohen, president of Employee Leasing of New York, a division of Cohen Personnel, says, "Companies are screaming for qualified people to fill entry-level jobs. Every day we receive hundreds of calls from banks, computer companies, and the like for help. The need for people at that level is dramatic. We have a thousand jobs we can't fill. Companies are even willing to send people to school for training and pick up the tuition." Says Cheryl Russell, "People in the baby bust generation who have job skills should be able to name their own tickets in the 1990s. On the other hand, businesses would be smart to upgrade the stature as well as the salaries of service and beginning jobs in order to attract better people." John Fanning, president of Uniforce Temporary Agency, with headquarters in New Hyde Park, Long Island, and sixty-five offices around the country, says, "The labor shortage in entry-level positions has killed the minimum wage—the minimum wage is dead. An interesting trend in this area is the hiring of older retired people to fill these jobs."

Changing Times magazine of November 1987 reports in an article on bright future careers:

Demographic changes will also affect job opportunities in the years ahead. Baby-boomers have always faced lots of competition from hordes of peers, but now that situation is being aggravated by companies cutting back on middle-management positions just as baby-boomers are ready to move into them, pushing even more career-switchers into the job market.

Ironically, the answer to the problem may also lie in demographics. Between 1986 and 2000, the number of new workers will expand by 18 percent, compared with 35 percent between 1972 and 1985. Such a dramatic swing won't necessarily create a labor shortage. Employers will be able to get work done by hiring part-time employees, automating their operations, or sending work to be done outside the country. But it should ease the pressure on job hunters.

However you look at it, the baby bust generation will have it made—but only if they're qualified. In the 1990s, people in their late twenties and thirties will be at premium.

What about the age groups just ahead of the baby boomers? What is the consumer orientation of the over-50s—their needs, desires, and pastimes? How do they differ from the baby boomers? *Modern Maturity* magazine, ostensibly geared to this group, sought answers to these questions in order to attract advertisers effectively and dispel the old assumptions and stereotypes of the over-50s as being "left behind." The magazine had a growing conviction that its readership was vital, vigorous, and committed to living a rich and full life. But it had to find a way to prove that to potential advertisers. The magazine hired the Daniel Yankelovich Group, Inc., to conduct a study comparing the values and behavior patterns of the over-50s with those of the baby boomers. The results were rewarding and surprising, finding more similarities between the groups than differences. Far from being "washed up," the over-50s are keeping step with the new and the innovative.

"One of the most striking findings of this research is the remarkable consistency between the values, attitudes, and consumer orientations of the 39-to-49 generation and their over-50 counterparts," the study reports. "This is a reflection of the diminishing values gap among all age groups in society. It suggests that the current 39-to-49 cohort does not differ markedly from the current 50-plus group, enabling marketers to plan strategies, introduce new products, and develop communications for those over 50 today without worrying that those strategies will become obsolete in a few years due to a 'generation gap.' This profile of the 50-plus population should remain stable for the next five to ten years.

Overall the study revealed:

1. The over-50 age group is no different from the immediately younger generation in its strongly held attitudes toward health and appearance. The approaches taken by the 50-and-over group to achieve the goals of looking and

feeling good are, overall, much the same as the younger cohort.

2. The outlook of the 50-and-over adults and their younger counterparts is also comparable in those issues and activities that relate to self-improvement and personal enrichment. They share a preference for productive use of leisure time rather than "play only," combining both aspects in such pursuits as cultural events, hobbies, and, in particular, travel.

3. Shopping strategies of the over-50 and under-50 men and women are very similar. Marketplace behavior patterns are quite alike, and so are attitudes toward price, quality, value, convenience, and service. A few differences do emerge, primarily related to spending practices: The 50-and-over group is more self-indulgent (e.g., more interested in spending on cars and clothing) and feels less pressured to buy new high-tech home appliances.

The implications of these findings are an invaluable guide to future marketers in their approach to the over-50 consumer.

1. Opportunities exist in categories that in the past were considered irrelevant for those relegated to the older group; for example, sophisticated fashion, home entertainment, mainstream food products (as opposed to remedy usages), personal care products such as cosmetics and fragrances, sports apparel and equipment, automobiles, and home technologies. Given the close correlation of the older group's values with those of the younger set, such assumptions are no longer valid.

2. Products should be created and positioned to appeal to the new self-image of 50-plus men and women. No special

treatment, then, is needed in non–age-related categories. Special approaches may be called for in behavioral or physiological areas, but not a different mind-set.

In essence, it is important for those targeting this group as consumers to be aware that, as opposed to the image of the past, the new and future middle-aged are active, not sedentary; socially involved and responsible, not withdrawn from the world; and have an overall positive attitude that reflects a sense of accomplishment.

The next significant groups among us are the newly old and the ever-increasing elderly. It will behoove the ambitious to analyze the needs of this marketplace. For instance, developers are now siting retirement communities through-out the country that differ markedly from the standard retirement centers of the past. The newly and future retired will be able to pick and choose the kind of living situation they prefer, from retirement villages in the Sunbelt to hotel-like living quarters in small communities. The Marriott Corporation, for example, currently is planning hotel-style communities for the elderly in metropolitan areas around the country. For a fixed fee and monthly payments, these communities will provide residents with food, shelter, medical care, and other services for life. A report on the plan in *American Demographics* of December 1983 notes that Marriott's target customers are elderly homeowners with incomes of at least $20,000 a year.

Since wobbly health usually accompanies aging, the health services field will flourish in the 1990s. Says William Flannagan, senior editor of *Forbes* magazine, "Two guys would stand to make more money by opening a nursing home than by investing in an MBA degree from any school less prestigious than the Ivy League brotherhood."

Lawrence Halpern of Dedham, Massachusetts, a registered investment advisor, publisher of *The Investment Pulse Newsletter*, former instructor at the Harvard Institute for Learning in Retirement, and currently a professor on the finance faculty of Providence College in Rhode Island, says, "In the 1990s, there will be a sizable need for financial planners to help prepare people for retirement as well as to help them after retirement to preserve their capital." Halpern also stresses that building and design consultants who specialize in accommodating the older population will be in demand.

Retirement homes, private schools, financial planning, innovative travel programs—whatever fulfills a particular need of a particular segment of the population will comprise the job wave of the 1990s. And the two givens in predicting America's social and economic future are the size of the baby boom market and the inevitable, inexorable graying of America.

CHAPTER 2

The Once and Future Economy

It is not only America's population that is changing. The baby boomers have grown up to Service America. Just as the country metamorphosed from an agricultural entity to a manufacturing monolith in the nineteenth century, so we have been involved in a transformation from manufacturing to services, a sort of postindustrial revolution.

The evidence is everywhere. The steel industry as a whole is suffering from a well-publicized decline, and the auto industry is beleaguered by overseas competition. Entire classes of middle managers and consultants have sprung up to provide advice and cope with our complicated doings with each other. The very label we attach to our era—the Information Age—is emblematic of our concerns. Not surprisingly, the baby boomers who flooded America's colleges and universities in the 1960s and 1970s emerged equipped not only with diplomas, but also with expectations of office jobs and substantial salaries. Blue-collar work has definitely gone out of vogue.

While this shift in attitude is at least partly a matter of conjecture, the statistics are not. Between 1900 and 1980, while the percentage of the nation's work force involved in agriculture dropped sharply from 37.6 percent to 2.8 percent, the manufacturing sector *also* declined overall, from 35.8 percent to 31.7 percent. Where have those workers gone? Into white-collar and service jobs, which together now account for 65.5 percent of all workers—more than double their 26.7 percent share in 1900. And estimates from the U.S. Bureau of Labor Statistics indicate that by 1995, a startling 71 percent of all American workers will pick up their paychecks at white-collar or service occupations.

But what, precisely, do we mean when we refer to "services"? The term can encompass a bewildering range of occupations and pursuits. The teenager who takes your order at McDonald's is a service worker; so is the management consultant paid by Union Carbide or CBS; so is Sting in concert (although his record albums fall into the realm of manufacturing). In Ron Albrecht and Karl Zemke's book *Service America*, insurance executive Ronald Kent Shelp of the American International Group specifies five categories of services, from least to most advanced:

1. *Unskilled personal services* (for instance, housekeeping, street vending).

2. *Skilled personal services* supporting industry and trade (skilled artisans, merchants, repair and maintenance workers).

3. *Industrial services* providing marketplace support (legal and accounting firms, banks, real estate brokers, insurance companies).

4. *Mass consumer services* catering to demand for discretionary services (travel agents, restaurateurs, actors and actresses, sports players, some health workers).

5. *High-technology business services*, drawing on advances
such as microchips and bioengineering to create and
streamline services (robotic technicians, management
consultants, university researchers, software
programmers).

The further we move into the service age, the more
sophisticated our service demands become, and the more
workers move into the last three categories.

None of this means, however, that manufacturing is
defunct, any more than the rise of industrialism brought
farming to a halt. Computers can only be constructed of
materials such as plastics and steel, which are made with
petroleum products and coal and ores, all of which requires
manpower. In fact, far from being in a decline, according
to David Birch, an MIT lecturer and president of Cognetics,
Inc., manufacturing is holding remarkably steady, merely
shifting from basic materials and midrange goods into more
innovative products such as computers and magazines aimed
at specialized markets (including everything from *50 Plus*
for older citizens to contest newsletters). But it does mean
that in terms of jobs—and especially fast-track, high-reward
jobs—service opportunities run away with the prize.

We are here, it seems, to serve, at least in the coming
decades. But how did we arrive here? There is nothing as
tangible as the baby boom bulge to provide a neat cause-
and-effect explanation; the reasons are myriad.

The greater our technological achievements, the more
jobs we eliminate, an equation that has carried particular
weight since the Industrial Revolution. The spinning jenny
could do the work of dozens of manual laborers in a fraction
of the time they required; similarly, in the modern garment
industry, laser-cutting techniques are further undercutting
the need for skilled seamstresses.

But jobs, like job-holders, rarely just disappear—they
move into other companies, other sectors of the economy.

In nineteenth-century England, the loss of jobs sparked the Luddite Rebellions during which rioting laborers attempted to destroy the threatening textile mills. Today, we've become accustomed to following those wayward, disappearing jobs wherever they may lead—and most of them are leading into the service sector. Those laser-cut blouses must still be advertised and marketed by people; the company that sells them relies on financial services consultants for its stock market dealings and on management analysts to help it run smoothly.

And those financial consultants and corporate advisors rely on computers and on information, information, information. High technology has done something much more earthshaking than eliminate jobs; it has fueled the information explosion. And the fallout continues to transform the way we live and do business.

Communications and computers: Those are the bywords of the Information Age. We are now dealers in ideas and information to whom esoteric or arcane knowledge is the most valuable commodity and speed of transmission or communication is the most valuable service. A huge number of people and businesses traffic directly or indirectly in information. There are the computer manufacturers such as Apple and IBM and Tandy; Lotus, Microsoft, and other devisers of programs that do everything from creating spreadsheets to editing documents to playing poker; the experts who train new users to work with the hardware and software. There are the movers of memos and packages like Fred Smith, the highly successful founder of Federal Express, and the telefax services. There are the editors and information specialists who gather facts and arrange them for effective presentation. And everywhere, there are the consultants who handle the problems of those who constantly handle information.

The world is a much smaller place than it once was. The Saturday morning cartoons that a Midwestern baby boomer watched as a child are largely the same as those recalled by the New Yorkers she met in college. A phone call instantly links friends who are an ocean apart, while an express mail service can transport some memento between them overnight. The stock market vagaries in New York cause frenzies of trading in Tokyo within hours, while many a New York market analyst starts his or her day with a phone call to a London counterpart.

The world is small enough, in fact, that to talk about the American economy by itself is akin to hollering down the old rain barrel to hear the echo—which is, in any case, being drowned out by all the loud conversations going on all around. We are part of a global economy, for better or worse. And that context is shaping the direction we are taking.

The continual filtering of jobs from one sector of the economy to another is not confined to the United States. If we are shifting largely to service, someone somewhere still has to be attending to the volume of manufacturing and production that these services support. And the print and television ads that are constantly appealing to our best consumer instincts (the majority of them created by American firms that fall into the service sector) are a dead giveaway: Hyundai cars and Goldstar video equipment from Korea, Panasonic computers and Sony stereos from Japan, along with Krups and Braun coffee grinders from Germany and Yugoslavian Yugos. The less well developed capitalist economies of the Pacific Rim, in particular, taking advantage of cheap labor and technology imported from the Western world, are able to deliver high-quality goods at low prices. Those countries that benefited most from U.S. aid after World War II are precisely the ones that now provide the strongest competition when it comes to products. That pressure has been a significant factor in pushing the United States toward services—of which we are now the world's leading purveyor, from banking to advertising. According to Department of Commerce statistics, although the country's balance of payments on trade in goods has dropped dizzyingly between 1970 and 1985 to a deficit of substantially more than $100 billion, the balance on trade in services has shown a steadily increasing surplus.

All of these factors, aided by wide-scale deregulation of a variety of industries including air transportation and banking, have helped set in motion a trend toward specialization and a "niche" economy. Businesses such as IBM that not long ago were perceived as unshakable megaliths are embattled or in states of extreme flux, and a flurry of mergers, takeovers forced and unforced, and split-offs have turned the big business picture into a kaleidoscope. And in the spaces between the pieces are very specific opportunities for those quick enough to catch sight of and fill them.

"The real growth in the future will be in the 'specialty niches' in every industry," Rosabeth Moss Kanter, a management consultant and professor at Harvard Business School, told *Working Woman* in July 1987. "Any company that produces a product or service that is unique, premium-priced, offers special value, and serves a booming market segment will be a growing business."

An enormous number of those successful companies will be small ones. The business climate of the United States has always been a balmy one for small start-ups—far more so than those of most European countries with their more restrictive regulations—and the entrepreneurial tradition has a strong hold on the American imagination. A poll conducted in 1986 by the public relations firm D'Arcy Masius Benton & Bowles revealed some startling results: For 38 percent of men and fully 47 percent of women, the "dream job" they would like to have is "head of own business."

The Fortune 500 companies that for years attracted all the fanfare in the business news are clearly only the tip of the economic iceberg. According to David Birch in *Job Creation in America*, of the 7 million or so companies that operate in the United States, nearly 90 percent are small firms that employ fewer than 20 workers. "Taken together," he writes, "these small companies create more jobs than the giants comprising the Fortune 500, grow more rapidly, run greater chances of failure, and show more adaptability." And these are the companies that will provide vast numbers of jobs, and especially fast-track jobs, in the coming decade.

These small companies have assorted advantages. They are flexible; they function particularly well by targeting specialized markets and ignoring (at least temporarily) those that fall outside their purview; they can offer a degree of quality control and attention to clients, particularly in the realm of services, that is very attractive and is often lacking in larger companies. They also can afford to take risks more readily than their biggest brothers. As the upper echelons of the book publishing industry are being consolidated, for instance—Macmillan now owns Scribners and Atheneum, Harper & Row's umbrella covers J.B. Lippincott, Random House and Alfred Knopf belong to an entity that also includes Rawson Associates and Pantheon—small publishing concerns are flourishing. Many so-called midlist authors, those who are known names but not blockbuster sellers and whose books usually are given relatively small print runs, are discovering that they fare far better at independent publishers which are not so locked into commercial success. Mystery writer Gregory Mcdonald, known for his detective Fletch, took his business to Boston's Hill & Wang after years in the "big leagues." David Leavitt, a bright light among the generation of up-and-coming young writers dubbed "the Young Turks," broke camp at Knopf and headed for the lure of a fat contract and a substantially larger print run at up-and-coming young Weidenfeld & Nicolson.

But if small is beautiful, big still carries a lot of weight. In an examination of information technology and the computer field in the 22 September 1987 *New York Times*, management consultant John Diebold of the Diebold Group predicted that mergers and erosion of profit margins will force many middle-sized companies out of business, while a few huge conglomerates and scores of small research-oriented firms will win the field. Reported the *Times*, "The middle companies will be vulnerable, Mr. Diebold explained, because they are neither big enough to do what giant companies can do nor flexible enough to do what tiny companies can."

That analysis, Birch's evidence shows, holds good for a much broader spectrum of the marketplace than computer-related jobs. Small companies have maneuverability, the capability to fill a specific need quickly and then adapt as that need changes. Large ones can draw on powerful corporate resources and name recognition, as well as their ability to acquire smaller businesses to accomplish their ends. Those in the middle must fight hard to keep from being squeezed out by these advantages at either end. They have, in a sense, outgrown their niches without yet having acquired the clout that accompanies size.

The niche mentality has filtered all the way up to the top. Beset by economic pressures, including those from overseas, corporations from the biggest, such as IBM and AT&T, on down have been forced to make drastic changes, trimming back wherever possible. These companies too are defining niches for themselves in two ways: They are narrowing their focus to the business of business and delegating other concerns, such as staff support and management analysis, to others; and they are targeting special areas into which to diversify—creating entire networks of "niche" holdings.

As noted before, corporations are increasingly likely to contract many of the services they use, from management to financial to public relations. If the Diebold Group handles management consulting, an accounting firm such as Price Waterhouse or Arthur Young deals with accounting and (as accounting houses are doing increasingly) with other financial matters, and Manning Selvage & Lee provides public relations know-how, the client company need not hire and provide benefits for all the staff who would once have carried out these tasks—a savings that solidly outweighs the fees paid to the consulting firms.

In fact, more and more companies are so enamored of the idea of being able to eliminate overhead costs relating to employees that they prefer not to hire their own staff at all, but to "lease" them. Since the 1950s, when the idea first arose, more than 350 employee-leasing businesses have been launched. These firms essentially act as independent personnel departments: They provide the employees— subject, of course, to the client's satisfaction—and take care of all the paperwork and details relating to health insurance, hiring, firing, and the like. The major difference, of course, is that the employees are actually working for the leasing firm. Presto—no more worries on the part of the client about retirement funds, severance packages, unemployment benefits. Well, not quite. No company can ever entirely escape such considerations. But certainly, an employee-leasing firm removes most of the day-to-day headaches and mitigates the cost.

One of the effects of this breakdown in the traditional corporate structure is the much-touted end of corporate loyalty. The parents and grandparents of the baby boomers expected, and with reason, that they would probably go to work for a company and, if their efforts were satisfactory, continue to work there indefinitely, perhaps for a lifetime. One could make a career out of being a Westinghouse man, or a Volrath salesman, or a secretary to Dr. Smith. Under such circumstances, loyalty came naturally, since the employer took care of a lifetime's worth of benefits and rewards.

But practically no one works for an employer for anything approaching a lifetime anymore, and practically none of the employers provide the benefits they once did. The ever more rapid rate of movement and change in the twentieth century has altered that as well. Cheryl Russell foresees in

100 Predictions for the Baby Boom that the average boomer will have ten—ten—different jobs during his or her productive years. Given a generous working life of some fifty years—from 18 to 68, say—that average amounts to a job change approximately every five years. To whom, then, does that employee's loyalty belong? And who merits the allegiance of a "leased" employee? The leasing company? The corporation for which the worker is providing services, but which does not directly pay the salary? The answer, as perceived by more and more people, is simple: One's primary loyalty is to oneself. A statement in the independent, entrepreneurial spirit, if there ever was one.

The flip side of the corporate "divestiture" of certain responsibilities and activities is the multiplication of small firms to take up that slack. The giant corporations and the smaller service firms exist symbiotically. Personnel jobs obviously haven't disappeared, but corporations are no longer the ideal place to look for them. Likewise, many service and information-related positions have moved into independent settings. In fact, many of the same workers who were laid off from corporate positions have simply transferred their expertise to consulting with the same sorts of companies they used to serve from the inside.

Corporations are fostering small companies in other ways as well. More and more of them are investing venture capital into start-up firms—to the tune of some $300 million in 1986, according to estimates by Venture Economics, Inc., an information services company. They are lured by two bonanzas: an average return on equity of 20 to 25 percent in those ventures that are successful, and the fruits of the technological innovations and other benefits that these small, research-oriented firms produce. The Xerox Corporation funneled money into Kurzweil Applied Intelligence, Inc., which has been working on computer-linked devices that can transcribe spoken English, in return for nonexclusive rights to Kurzweil's technology. General Electric has made a lucrative habit of investing venture funds into a number of companies, including two small computer firms. Eastman Kodak often sinks its venture capital funds into companies that are trying out ideas which originated internally at Kodak; if the start-ups are successful, Kodak may then buy the company and its product.

These small firms accomplish two objectives for their investors: They provide an entrepreneurial atmosphere unhindered by too much bureaucracy and managerial restriction, and they take risks that a more unwieldy, more conservative corporation might not take of itself. And they also provide the sort of diversification into niches and specialized areas that is so vital to the corporations.

Change and adaptation, as David Birch notes in *Job Creation*, are essential: ". . . nonentrepreneurial firms are the most likely to go out of business. . . . *non-risk takers are among the most likely candidates for liquidation.*" This is as true for large as for small firms. The large ones simply tend to accomplish their entrepreneuring by proxy and by spreading out their investments across a broad spectrum. Thus one sees Coca-Cola getting into moviemaking by buying Columbia Pictures, Gulf+Western diversifying into publishing (among other things), and Sears, Roebuck & Company acquiring the stockbrokering firm of Dean Witter and the real estate brokerage Coldwell Banker.

The bottom line is that the small companies are the grist that drives the economy and, at least in part, the soon-to-be postindustrial giants. Considering that the rate of new incorporations continues to accelerate, as it has done for nearly forty years, it is clear where the majority of job opportunities will be in the 1990s.

What does all this mean in terms of individual outlook?

Small companies are far more fertile ground for new jobs, and especially for fast-track jobs, than large ones. The biggest corporations will continue to account for a substantial segment of the work force and provide valuable experience for would-be entrepreneurs, but the vast majority of positions are found in small firms—and these offer unmatched opportunities for shaping oneself to take advantage of the demands of the moment.

High-end service sector jobs offer far more promise than those in manufacturing. Again, simply by sheer weight of numbers, and because of the growth potential in this area that manufacturing has not been able to match, jobs in service offer a surer road to fast-track success.

Whether in manufacturing or service, the most successful companies and careers are those that identify a niche or special need and fill it. Health products and services aimed at the over-85 population, magazines for baby boom women having children, financial planning for baby boom families coping with school tuition and their aging parents' health bills: These are the sorts of things that will take off.

The most successful workers and companies are those that fill a niche but are not confined by it. In other words, portable skills are absolutely essential. Rapid change is the hallmark of our time, and dealing with it effectively is the hallmark of the successful fast-tracker. Says David Birch in *Job Creation,* "Those who are unaware . . . and rigid about change will suffer the most, usually to the degree of their rigidity and ignorance. To succeed means getting accustomed to the idea of multiple jobs and careers and a willingness to move and shift." And an ability to shift. Chemical engineers with only traditional training, for instance, were at a disadvantage during the hiring crunch of the early 1980s; those who had additional expertise in computers or another field had more to offer an employer and more options.

Choose a company rather than an industry. Although the vast majority of opportunities will occur in service, and in particular areas of service, that doesn't rule out the rest of the job market. In fact, some of the most exciting and challenging openings are in just those fields that seem to be doing the worst. Enormously successful Florida Steel put new backbone in its sagging industry. Reebok's aerobic shoes have proved that the U.S. shoe industry still has some kick left in it. Opportunities are where you find them.

KNOWING THE SCORE

A basic understanding of the forces that are likely to influence the job market is crucial, but that alone doesn't guarantee success. Opportunities in the medical field may abound, but one doctor builds a thriving practice while another seems to be constantly on the verge of bankruptcy. Thousands of entrepreneurs every year take advantage of the conducive business climate to start new companies, yet the vast majority of them fail.

What makes one career fizzle, while another sizzles? It is seldom a matter of the career itself—there are success stories even in the struggling manufacturing sector—but of knowing how to angle into it. Certain factors play a determining role in shaping any career for success, no matter what the field. And above all, contending on the fast track requires a commitment of attention and dedication.

_____

_____

_____

_____

_____

_____

_____

_____

CHAPTER 3

What Adds Up to a Fast-Track Career?

In every career there are a variety of choices to be made: whom to work for, which promotions or job offers to accept, how to handle a new situation or trend, and so on. And these are the sorts of decisions on which fast-track success rests. How to determine what constitutes such success? The following scenarios offer some guidelines.

CASE 1

The opportunities in personnel staffing are proliferating in the 1990s as never before. Making the most of these opportunities depends on correctly identifying and taking advantage of the trends.

Stephen Ellison, at 38, is director of personnel at a large independent computer information company. He has been there for twelve years, having worked up from personnel

screener to his present prestigious job. A conscientious
worker, he has kept his knowledge of the computer field
current, and his contacts are extensive. In the last year,
Ellison's company has been leasing some employees from
a staff-leasing agency. He is aware that fewer employees
are working directly under his auspices.

His company assures him that his job is not in danger,
but in fact adds other responsibilities outside personnel work
to his department. Ellison weighs his situation. Although
he is qualified as an expert computer science recruiter, he
comes down on the side of security and the familiar and
stays at his job.

Peter Trent is a 40-year-old university campus recruiter
for a major utility company. His specialty is hiring good
computer science people. His job experience for the past
fifteen years has been in some area of personnel and
information. Because of the nature of his current work, Trent
is singularly attuned to the competitive market when it comes
to recruiting top computer-trained people. His contacts and
his knowledge of the field and the needs of the industry
equal those of Ellison.

Trent assesses his qualifications, evaluates the opportunities and direction of the market, and decides on a career
change. He joins an executive recruitment agency as a
"headhunter" specializing in placing top systems analysts
and computer programmers. The job is personally challenging, in that Trent has a quota to fill and works on commission.

Which of them is more likely to move onto the fast track?
It is Peter Trent who has crossed over into the fast lane
where demand outweighs supply. Let's eliminate the
ostensible personality differences between the two men,
which are at best misleading. On first take it would seem
that Ellison is afraid of change and unwilling to take a risk.
Trent, on the other hand, appears adventuresome. Nothing
is further from the truth.

Stephen Ellison has curtailed his career on several counts.
He has failed either to acknowledge or interpret accurately

the growth direction of the personnel field. By choosing to stay where he is, he has overlooked or misread the major change in the structure of personnel staffing—namely, the advent and success of employee leasing and contract staffing agencies. The expansion of this type of agency has changed the basic concept of the employer's involvement and participation in hiring employees. Because essentially the employees work for the agency and not for the company, personnel departments in many companies are being phased out. This trend was evident in his own company's policy of hiring some employees from an employee leasing firm. In substance, Ellison is the risk-taker. He ignored the dead-end aspect of his job and the strong possibility of being phased out. In addition, he did not assess his special qualifications. Given his expertise in the thriving computer science field and his experience in personnel, Ellison was well positioned to move into a more lucrative and secure niche in his profession.

Peter Trent, on the other hand, has seen the picture clearly. He chose to move from a job that is secure but limited to one that is not only secure but growing. Trent has assessed his combined areas of expertise and sized up the opportunity to combine them into an expanding and lucrative career. As a headhunter specializing in computer science, he stands to receive between 25 and 30 percent of a year's salary for every applicant he places. He has made an excellent move in the direction of filling an ever increasing need on the part of business, as well as switching over from a fixed income to, in all likelihood, a constantly escalating one.

CASE 2

Prospects in dentistry have been mixed in recent years, as the closing of several dental schools attests. But in this field, as in the other health professions, demand will never entirely disappear; success depends on targeting it correctly.

Two young classmates in their twenties, Jake Davison and Susan Wells, fresh from their lengthy and expensive tenure in dental school, face the challenge of establishing themselves in practice. Both are aware of the difficulties but have high hopes of success.

Dr. Davison went into dentistry with the idea of specializing in treatment for children. He knows that rates of tooth decay among children have dropped dramatically in the last decades, due, ironically enough, to the dental industry's own success and to fluoridation. However, he assesses the situation and decides that the need for dental work is likely to remain fairly constant henceforth. He further concludes that the openings are most promising outside metropolitan areas. Obeying this judgment and a yen for independence, he opens a brand-new office in his hometown in Indiana and hangs out his shingle. He advertises himself as a family dentist with expertise in handling children and begins to seek customers among the school community.

Dr. Wells studies her options and, daunted by her debts and the costs of an independent practice, relinquishes the idea of working on her own. Instead, she accepts an offer to join an established dental clinic in a New Jersey suburb near New York City as a junior partner to several other practitioners. Although this clinic treats a variety of patients, young and old, for a variety of problems, its specialty is cosmetic dentistry, for which it recently invested in a computer system and appropriate graphics software. Dr. Wells will receive training on this equipment. She would prefer to remain near New York City, but, as one of the conditions of her acceptance, she is aware that she may be asked to transfer to one of the new branch offices the clinic is considering setting up in outlying New Jersey communities.

Which of the two new dentists is on the road to success? Dr. Wells, for a number of reasons.

Dr. Davison is laboring under several disadvantages. First of all, although it may not decline further, dentistry among children is not likely to be one of the most rewarding specialties in the next few years. Certainly, there will always be a need for checkups and filling the occasional cavity, but these have become too occasional to offer Dr. Davison much chance of skyrocketing to remarkable success. Nor has he chosen another area of specialization to balance against his first preference; his focus is too narrow. He is on target in selecting a somewhat rural area for his particular specialty, an area where fewer dentists are willing to move, but his independent practice may well become the proverbial albatross. Dr. Davison must assume alone the prohibitive burden of malpractice insurance, equipment, and overhead—which is likely to prevent him from keeping up with future advances in technology that will give competitors an edge.

Dr. Wells, by contrast, has a definite competitive advantage. She has minimized the costs of insurance and overhead by joining forces with a number of other dentists in an established practice. Furthermore, the clinic she has chosen is capitalizing on what is one of the most lucrative, fastest-growing trends in the field: aesthetic dentistry. Its location, too—in the New York metro area—allows it to tap a huge local market for this type of work. The clinic's computer system not only provides up-to-the-minute technology for cosmetic dentistry, but can link the clinic with other dental offices and databases for up-to-the-minute information. And even if Dr. Wells transfers to another location, she will still remain part of the clinic's network and enjoy many of its benefits.

CASE 3

Few arenas are as alluring as the financial sector in all its permutations, with its possibilities of high rewards in the short term. But few are as risky or as volatile.

Alice Powell, 33, possessed of an MBA from Harvard, has spent several years in the financial services sector, specializing in municipal bonds for a large Manhattan investment firm. She has been promoted twice, most recently about two years ago, and she hopes to be considered for a managerial position that is likely to open up soon. Meanwhile, she receives an offer from a rival firm that would entail shifting into securities analysis. After consideration, she rejects the outside offer, deciding that refining her knowledge of municipal bonds will make her more indispensable to her current employer; besides, she does not want to give up the prospect of promotion to a managerial position.

Thirty-year-old Albert Deever used his MBA from New York University to land a job as a securities analyst. Like Alice Powell, he works for a major Wall Street investment firm, and he has been promoted once. Feeling less sanguine about his chances for continued promotion, however, he diverts some of his attention away from securities and starts to take classes on the side with the goal of becoming a certified public accountant as well. He hopes that this additional knowledge, though perhaps less glamorous than his original field and though it has taken some of his energy away from securities work, will count in his favor when it comes to advancement.

Although their positions may sound similar, of the two Albert Deever is in much the better position. Why?

Both Ms. Powell and Mr. Deever are susceptible to changes in the market, and particularly to layoffs as invest- ment and brokerage firms react to the pinch of financial downswings. The 1980s saw career bloodbaths in both the municipal bond and securities analysis fields. However, the securities analysts emerged in much better shape. Many were able to take their knowledge to the other side of the fence and join the very companies whose securities they had previously been analyzing; these firms hired them on the premise that such expertise would pay off in strategic planning or other areas. Municipal bond specialists, however, were largely unable to take advantage of similar opportunities—their knowledge was of little use to most corporations, and few municipalities dealing with bond issues required such experts either. And Alice Powell has put herself in the position of having no other viable alternative. Although specialized knowledge can be quite valuable, there is definitely such a thing as becoming too specialized—as she may painfully find out.

Deever's self-education program, on the other hand, is likely to pay off handsomely, either in itself or as a means of moving into financial planning. Although accounting might seem more mundane than some of the sophisticated stock market operations, it is a field that at the moment seems to know no limits. The need for accounting and financial planning never wanes; in fact, the more volatile the financial environment, the more call there is for such assistance. Many accounting and financial services companies have expanded to include tax and retirement planning and the like, in addition to more traditional corporate and personal accounting. And changes in the tax laws increase the demand.

Furthermore, Albert Deever's versatility is likely to set him on the path to promotion more quickly than Alice Powell, especially if he possesses good writing and communications skills. Although companies hire specialists to fill specialized niches, they tend to prefer people with a broader or more general background for their middle- and upper-level management positions.

CASE 4

The traditional precept that "money is in sales" will still hold true in the 1990s. For good salespersons, selling has always been one of the highest-paying careers. However, the future of sales is changing shape in an important way.

After college, Hugh Rogers had joined his father's business as a junior traveling salesman for a large apparel firm. His father had worked as a salesman for the company for some thirty years. Upon his father's death, young Rogers was offered and took over his father's complete selling territory. In the two years he has been a senior salesman, Rogers has noticed a change in the apparel industry. More and more companies are establishing manufacturer-owned shops within large department stores. These in-store boutiques are often staffed by the clothing makers' own employees. Rogers realizes, correctly, that the traditional salespersons in the industry are being eased out. In fact, they still exist really only to service the accounts. He decides to leave the apparel industry and look for a selling job in another field.

Judy Ridgeway, a few years out of college, has chosen fashion and sales as a career. She is offered a job as sales representative for an old-time, successful coat manufacturing company. The firm is solid, with some long-held prestige. On close examination of the industry, Judy becomes aware of the trend toward "verticalization" and that more and more it is the top managers who clinch the deals when manufacturers sell to big department stores. In her continuing job search, Judy is offered a job as a "field representative" for a multifaceted designer company. The job would include merchandising their in-store boutiques and consulting with the stores on promotion and retail sales. Judy Ridgeway chooses to become a field representative, a position that is salaried as opposed to commissioned.

Is Hugh Rogers or Judy Ridgeway on the way to a fast-track career? Judy Ridgeway is the long-term winner here. Let's see why.

Although Hugh Rogers has read the vane correctly, he has made an unimaginative choice by failing to explore the potential of the new and innovative method of selling and marketing in the apparel industry in the 1990s. By seeing himself only as a salesman, Rogers has put a lid on his career vision.

As for Judy Ridgeway, she has moved over into a new wave of selling and increased her potential for advancement in the field. Not only do her options allow her to move up to top management, but she has widened her area of expertise in her chosen field.

So, what constitutes a fast-track career? Every profession, of course, is different, and each instance within a given profession will have its own defining details. However, the success stories across the board have certain aspects in common. The four fast-trackers described here were astute enough not only to spot trends in their fields, but to interpret their direction correctly—and then to take advantage of them. Each of these careers rests on new, strong trends within a field and generally on serving a specific need. Also, each of these careers is on a path that expands choices rather than restricts them; these four people have all acted to augment their expertise. Clearly, a fast-track career relies on awareness, accurate judgment, an ability to adapt or shift, and the maximization of advantageous choices.

CHAPTER 4

Is a Fast-Track Career Right for You?

According to Dr. Francis X. Clifton, director of the Center for International Living and private practitioner of psychotherapy, individuals with successful fast-track temperaments have two essential traits. First, they exhibit intense "willfulness," which is coupled with active intelligence and intuition; in other words, they are driven to put into form or practice whatever they plan out. Second, fast-trackers have an internal sense of time that is directed to the present moment. They do not hold onto feelings or memories and are more likely to look to the future for a solution than to the past.

The following test, developed by Dr. Clifton, will help you to determine whether you have a fast-track temperament. If you agree strongly with a statement, give yourself 4 points;

if you generally agree, 3 points; if you disagree somewhat, 2 points; if you strongly disagree, 1 point.

1. I enjoy taxing and difficult tasks. _____
2. I do not need much sleep when I am engrossed in a project. _____
3. I need to complete what I start. _____
4. I am often accused of being domineering. _____
5. I am quick, decisive, and energetic. _____
6. Perceiving new trends and possibilities comes easily to me. _____
7. I don't let feelings interfere with work. _____
8. I can be characterized as an explorer. _____
9. I am not a collector. _____
10. When I leave one job for another, I don't look back. _____
11. My future depends on me. _____

If your score on questions 1 through 6 is between 18 and 24 points, you are willful and active; these are primary components of a fast-tracker. If you scored highly within this section but did not top 11 for questions 7 to 11, you probably get too caught up in feelings or emotions to have the adaptability required of a successful fast-tracker.

A score of 15 to 20 on the last six questions indicates that your time is your own and feelings do not interfere with your completing a task. If you scored between 36 and 46 combined, you can consider yourself a person who achieves, succeeds, and then leaves—but most likely you already know this about yourself.

A NEW LOOK AT THE OLD PROFESSIONS

The need for medical attention, legal advice, and engineering know-how is ever with us, and if anything on the increase. However, the nature of the needs are shifting along with the changes in the population profile, economy, technology, and priorities of the country.

For those of you considering or just entering or already in a profession, it is essential to study the emphasis, trends, and new opportunities in your field in order to choose or shift into the niche which best serves your interest and career. A careful look at where the professions are headed in the 1990s can make the difference between being sought after and in-the-swim, and treading water in the sea of obsolescence.

CHAPTER 5

A New Look at the Old Professions

MEDICINE AND HEALTH CARE

As always, medicine and health care are top priority professions—prestigious and lucrative. We continue to battle against the ever present threats of disease and health deterioration; the fronts and the emphasis may shift, but the war goes on. Career opportunities abound, but they have changed from those of the last decade and continue to change in accordance with health needs, disease prominence, and, more important, with the present interpretation of the health field.

In the past two decades we have seen the dependable family GP and the accepted routine of house calls all but disappear, and the corresponding ascendancy of the specialist and office visits. This new pattern still holds—but now some of the old specialties are diminishing while new ones are becoming more prominent. It is easy to see the relationship between baby boomers delaying parenthood and limiting their number of children to the narrowing need for obstetricians and pediatricians. And in the arena of disease, well-known scourges are conquered only to be replaced by new ones. In past times, the medical profession was burdened with diphtheria, tuberculosis, and polio. Today, doctors and health-care personnel are plagued by the three As: Alzheimer's, AIDS, and aging. Each of these requires special training and knowledge and is becoming a more and more specialized field unto itself. Cancer, which remains unabated, became a specialty in much the same way. More often than not, cancer patients are treated by oncologists.

This is not to say that, if you have the calling, you must choose a specialty on the basis of demand alone, but it is a consideration. These areas of specialization apply to nurses as well as other health-care professionals, including research scientists and lab and procedure technicians, such as those who handle X-rays and radiation.

By far the most significant change and trend in medicine is the acknowledged attitude that Medicine is Business. This does not necessarily mean that business offsets dedication, but it does take into account pragmatic concerns such as assessing financial and lifestyle opportunities. Doctors are weighing the pros and cons of group practice against those of one-person private practice. They are looking into the advantages of ownership of or partnership in physician-owned outpatient clinics and nursing homes. MDs and other health-field people who are interested in administrative positions are securing MBAs.

There is a steadily climbing need in the health "industry" for people who combine business know-how with medical expertise. According to authors Walecia Konrad and Joan Tedeschi in an article entitled "The 25 Hottest Careers of 1987" that appeared in *Working Woman* magazine (May 1987), "Experts predict the demand for 'business doctors' will

quickly outpace demand for physicians in private practice—
an already saturated field in many areas." Mary Gianni,
executive director of the Center for Career Service at
Columbia University, believes this saturation of private-
practice physicians will level out. Her figures indicate a sharp
decrease in medical school enrollments. She believes the
face-value reason is twofold: Students are afraid of the high
malpractice insurance rates and are disillusioned because
the community's exalted image of the doctor has sharply
deteriorated. But although doctoring may no longer appear
in such a glamorous light, Gianni believes that is not the
primary reason for the drop-off; the real reason, as she sees
it, is that today's students are impatient to make good money
and are not willing to put in the time and hard work necessary
to become a physician. It would seem that, for many, ambition
precludes delayed money.

However, those with the calling or inclination will find
that this view is both somewhat crass and short-sighted, failing
to take into account the obvious career opportunities in the
field. Dr. Mary Anne Devanna, research director at Columbia
University's Management Institute and director of executive
education at the Graduate School of Business, predicts,
"Health-care careers across the board will flourish and
escalate in financial rewards and niche needs. The Bureau
of Labor Statistics forecasts that during the next several years,
one of nine new jobs in the U.S. will be health-related. The
BLS also predicts that by the year 2000, for every seven
physicians in the U.S., there will be five or six nonclinical
health-care professionals also working in the field."

"Now is a particularly good time to enter this industry,"
advises Anne Kahl, a BLS analyst and project leader. "Health
care is in a period of major transition; it is a perfect time
to get in on the ground floor."

In the same report mentioned above, the BLS notes the
nation's nursing shortage. One profession that needs more
people power is nursing. The nation's 1.4 million registered

nurses will have to increase 44 percent, to 2 million by the year 2000, in order to meet demand. And the 631,000 licensed practical nurses will have to increase 37 percent, to 869,000.

These figures notwithstanding, it is predicted that by the year 2000, only about 40 to 45 percent of nurses will be in a hospital setting, compared with 69 percent today. Some nurses have already jumped the gun on this prediction, contributing to the current shortage in hospitals. Many nurses have left hospitals for better jobs elsewhere—in nursing homes, in corporate medical offices, in health maintenance organizations, as visiting nurses and school nurses, and in other community service jobs—often with higher pay and more convenient hours. Some nurses are acquiring advanced degrees so that they can teach or enter research, and others work for drug companies in such fields as marketing. Laurie Giovinazzo, head oncology nurse at St. Vincent's Hospital on Staten Island, says that several of her colleagues have become lawyers. Nurse-lawyers are assured of a successful practice by representing doctors facing malpractice and in other legal matters involving medical problems such as personal injury accidents.

All the indications—from the demographic changes of an older America to the leap in medical technology and services, along with the change from the spare-no-expense health-care mentality to the current strictly business/cost-cutting emphasis—ensure that health-care career opportunities both clinical and nonclinical will soar.

Those who meet the primary prerequisite for choosing the medical field—namely, a true liking for or inclination toward the healing profession—will find some particularly rewarding opportunities in the following areas and disciplines.

PHYSICIAN

Doctors' incomes continue to be, on average, among the highest in the country. The AMA reported that between 1986 and 1987, the mean income of physicians rose 6.5 percent to almost $120,000 annually. Today's physicians, however, are faced with professional and financial decisions that in the past were either nonexistent or irrelevant. The automatic avenues and access into private practice that new doctors once enjoyed have become more complicated. With big business entering the health-care field in the form of corporate-owned hospital chains and clinics, government regulations on health insurance allowances, and the skyrocketing cost of state-of-the-art medical equipment, new doctors are restricted in choices and have lost some of their sovereignty.

Does this mean the opportunities in medicine have diminished? No! There are plenty of opportunities; they have merely changed. For those of you entering the profession or looking to switch, it is important to be aware of the changes and future trends.

New doctors have to consider carefully their choice of specialty and the area in which to practice. In addition, a choice must be made between individual practice, joining another doctor as a junior partner, or working for either a health maintenance organization or on the staff of a hospital or clinic. Other options for a new doctor include research, teaching, and working for a corporation or the government.

New York Times reporter Elizabeth M. Fowler wrote in her Careers column of 2 February 1988 that Glaxo Inc., a North Carolina pharmaceutical company, has instituted a program to help third-year medical students select a specialty using real-world facts. Dr. Stuart Bondunant, dean of the University of North Carolina School of Medicine and a member of the advisory group that worked on the program, called it "not a quick fix," but "a process for making better decisions."

The Glaxo Pathway Evaluation Program, a three-hour workshop, helps students assess their personal characteristics against norms for various medical specialties. As to real-world facts, the workshop provides information about which specialties will be in short supply in the 1990s and which geographical areas will have the most opportunities. According to Glaxo, specialties where shortages are expected include: anesthesiology, oncology, emergency medicine, hematology, physical medicine and rehabilitation, preventive medicine, psychiatry, sports medicine, and geriatrics.

In contrast, areas such as gynecology and obstetrics, pediatrics, cardiology, pulmonary diseases, and ophthalmology will be oversupplied in the 1990s.

Dr. Robert La Penna, a third-year resident at St. Vincent's Hospital on Staten Island, has chosen internal medicine as his specialty. He is one of the growing number of physicians who are combining their personal needs with community needs.

"I thought of becoming a gastroenterologist—a sub-specialty of internal medicine—but realized I wanted a continuing and close relationship with patients," he observes. "Besides, there is a dire need for primary care physicians. By the 1990s, there will be a deficit of internists. In a lot of areas we have a surplus of specialists."

A survey by the National Resident Matching Program in Evanston, Illinois, bears Dr. La Penna out. The survey as reported by Dr. Lawrence K. Altman in the *New York Times* of 19 April 1988, found that the numbers of positions offered in three-year residency programs in internal medicine has exceeded the number of U.S. medical school graduates who choose this specialty. Part of the gap has been met by foreign medical school graduates.

Internists diagnose disease and usually assume continuing care for patients who call on them for a myriad of ailments, ranging from arthritis to AIDS. There is little question that more internists will be needed as more AIDS cases are diagnosed.

The move away from primary care fields—such as internal medicine, family practice, and pediatrics—toward a more technological practice with less doctor–patient contact is an indication of the medical economics for the 1990s as well as a choice in lifestyle. Anesthesiologists and radiologists, for example, generally earn more money with less night and weekend duty. The AMA reported that income increases from 1986 to 1987 varied widely among specialists, with radiologists enjoying the largest, a growth of 17 percent, to an average income of $168,000, while family practice physicians saw a rise of only 3 percent, to $80,300 annually.

Dr. Gerald Bresner, a New Jersey podiatrist who specializes in foot surgery, says, "The fastest growing surgical sub-specialty is same-day surgery. Hernia, cataract, and foot operations are all being done on an in-and-out basis. Most times it is not necessary for patients to stay in the hospital overnight. Besides, insurance companies are more flexible about procedures that do not involve surgical stays. So, same-day surgery is ultimately less of a hassle for the surgeon, and it's more profitable."

Dr. Bresner, who has two offices in New Jersey, says that many doctors who are in sub-specialties are getting together and buying small hospitals and turning them into same-day surgery centers. "Doctors can't be strictly doctors any more," he notes. "They have to understand the business of medicine, as well."

Apparently, Dr. Bresner chose his sub-specialty wisely. The Bureau of Labor Statistics rates podiatry as number 14 on its list of the 25 fastest-growing jobs for the years 1985–1995. Bressner says it is due to the growth in sports medicine, jogging, and the general fitness craze.

From all indications, opportunities and financial rewards will continue to grow in doing X-ray and other diagnostic procedures. Medical procedures that used to be done only in hospitals are now being done by private physicians who are trained in the procedure and have chosen it as their specialty.

In an article in the *New York Times*, Milt Freudenheim points out that other expanding medical areas are psychiatry, alcohol and drug abuse treatment, and physical rehabilitation. Demand for rehabilitation doctors and therapists is due to demographic trends, notably the aging of our population. Aging brings with it a greater incidence of such chronic disabilities as strokes, arthritis, and hip fractures.

These needs are reflected in the increase in for-profit specialty hospitals. In 1987, the Hospital Corporation of America sold more than 100 general hospitals while investing heavily in psychiatric hospitals. Other hospital chains, such as National Medical Enterprises Inc. and a number of small chains, are expanding their facilities for alcohol and drug abuse therapy, physical rehabilitation, and treatment of Alzheimer's disease. According to the Federation of American Health Systems, more than one-third of the 1,375 for-profit hospitals in the country are now exclusively for specialties such as psychiatric care—including treatment of depression, schizophrenia, and phobias; substance abuse; or rehabilitation. The trend toward specialty hospitals results from federal medicare restrictions establishing set fees for treatment of specific illnesses. This caused a loss of revenues for general hospitals, as patients were discharged after shorter stays.

For those of you going into medicine, the direction is clear and the opportunities varied. The current and future health problem areas are pinpointed and are based on demographics, medical and social diseases, and economic trends. The profession of medicine remains noble, secure, and profitable.

PHYSICIAN EXECUTIVES

The need for physician executives is another strong growth opportunity, according to an article in *Working Women* magazine in July 1987.

> Physician executives are helping hospitals, HMOs, and other health-care facilities to cope with runaway costs. They act as liaisons between physicians and management to find more efficient ways to care for

the sick without sacrificing quality. Generally, physician executives must earn an MD and complete a three-year residency. They also must be pros at financial analysis, accounting, economics, marketing, and strategic-planning—subjects they master while studying for the MBA, master of hospital administration, or master of public health. Executives with an MD, residency, and MBA start at about $75,000 and jump into six-figure salaries within a few years.

NURSING

Does nursing seem a rather prosaic choice of careers? All the better, according to Neal Rosenthal, chief of the Labor Department's Division of Occupational Outlook. "If someone asked me whether his son or daughter should train to be a lunar miner or a nurse, I'd say nurse," Rosenthal remarked to *Changing Times* magazine, warning against a tendency to plan one's future around fanciful forecasts of jobs that may or may not exist someday. The same article (November 1987) reports that nursing appears on the government's list of occupations expected to grow much faster than average in the 1990s.

Registered nurses in the 1990s will be able to choose among an ever increasing variety of career alternatives in and out of the hospital setting. As cost containment and diagnostic related groups (DRGs) encourage hospitals to discharge patients sicker and quicker, more and more nurses are needed to provide home and ambulatory care. As Americans live longer, the demand for RNs increases in nursing homes and extended-care facilities. With third-party payers and government regulators tightening their grip on health care, more nurses are also needed for discharge planning and utilization review.

According to the 1988 issue of *Nursing Opportunities*, experienced nurses are already taking full advantage of changes in the health-care industry to establish new careers outside the hospital setting. The following list, drawn from

Nursing Opportunities 1988, offers a breakdown of non-hospital options.

Home health care. The number of home-care nurses, although still relatively small, is growing at a rapid pace. The majority of these nurses are employed by private agencies, nonprofit health services, or hospital-affiliated agencies. Many home health agencies require a BSN, at least one year of hospital med/surg experience, and IV certification.

To be an effective home-care nurse, one must be independent and self-reliant, since there isn't a hospital team to fall back on for support. Working hours in home care may be more appealing than hospital hours, but be prepared for weekend coverage and 24-hour responsibility for your caseload. Salary and benefits are usually comparable to those offered by hospitals.

Nursing agencies. RNs who sign up with agencies have a measure of flexibility and independence and gain a wide range of experience in different practice settings. The typical agency will provide temporary staffing for hospitals, doctors' offices, HMOs, and other health-care facilities. It may also provide nurses for home health care and private duty. Most agencies cover a limited geographical area, though a few are regional, national, or even international. You'll have the freedom to choose your own assignments, depending on your level of experience, the variety of services provided by the agency, and the hours and days that you want to work.

Nurses in this area usually need at least a year of hospital med/surg experience. Some agencies require CPR certification and other skills. Pay depends on the assignment but is usually higher than you'd receive as a hospital staff nurse.

On the other hand, job security and fringe benefits are minimal.

Private-duty nursing. Nurses who choose private duty are self-employed; they function as private practitioners. They're hired by a patient or his/her family to take care of the patient in a hospital or at home. Ordinarily, they care for only one or two patients at a time. Like home-care nurses, private-duty nurses must be self-confident and reliable. They need good assessment skills as well as the ability to work alone, without a team for support. Private-duty nurses usually sign up with a registry or hospital, which provides the assignments.

Physicians' offices. Nurses who work in doctors' offices often perform clerical as well as educational and clinical duties. Experience in a hospital or other clinical area is usually required, and a background in public health is useful. Working in a doctor's office is generally less stressful than working in a hospital. The hours are regular, but you may find yourself putting in evenings and weekends in this time of increased competition for patients. Pay tends to be lower than it is in hospitals, and fringe benefits are variable.

Ambulatory care centers. Fast, convenient service is the attraction of these facilities, which combine features of a doctor's office and a hospital's emergency room. Excellent assessment skills are essential here, as is the ability to apply them to an enormous variety of problems. You'll make follow-up phone calls to check on a patient's progress, so your communication skills must be excellent, too.

In many centers, a year or two of hospital ICU or ER experience is required. Salaries are competitive with entry-level hospital positions, but benefits may not be as good. Hours are generally flexible.

Nursing homes. RNs who work in nursing homes help elderly patients or patients needing rehabilitation adjust to the effects of aging, disability, chronic illness, surgery, and trauma. The staff may be made up mostly of LPNs, nursing assistants, and aides, with RNs providing guidance and supervision. This means you'll need leadership and organizational skills. Salaries traditionally have been lower than those in hospitals. The working hours are similar.

Hospices. As the number of elderly and terminally ill patients increases, so will the demand for hospice nurses. A hospice makes it possible for a patient to die at home, or it can provide comfortable, homelike surroundings in which the patient can spend his/her last days or weeks. Duties include keeping the patient comfortable physically and psychologically, teaching the family how to care for him/ her, and providing support for members of the family.

Some hospices want their nurses to have a BSN degree, but most of them require only a few years of nursing experience. The majority of hospice nurses visit an average of four patients a day and work regular hours. Typically, a hospice nurse is on call one night a week and one weekend out of every six or seven.

Nurses working for hospices affiliated with hospitals can expect pay that's comparable to that of a hospital staff nurse. Nurses employed by independent hospices, which are usually run by home health agencies, may earn slightly less.

Public health. Local health departments and certain nonprofit community organizations such as the American Cancer Society hire nurses as providers of direct care, consultants, and advisors. A nurse in public health generally needs a BSN. Working hours are regular, but the pay is generally lower than that of a hospital job.

Occupational health care. A number of companies hire nurses to monitor the health and safety of their employees.

Nurses in such a position are responsible for on-the-job health care, counseling, emergency care, wellness and health maintenance programs, education, and risk management. A background in public health is usually necessary. It's also helpful to have a master's degree in occupational health and some knowledge of industrial chemicals and toxins.

Working hours usually coincide with the company's hours of operation, which in some factories may mean the midnight shift. Responsibilities may also include making follow-up home visits after regular hours. In general, the salaries are comparable to hospital pay.

School nursing.   In elementary, secondary, and postsecondary institutions, school nurses provide testing and diagnostic services and direct care to students. Additionally, they may find themselves teaching health classes and giving safety and first-aid seminars, as well as conducting physical exams and counseling students. Many states require a school nurse to have a BSN with special certification and additional education in public health. The salary is about the same as hospital pay but covers only the academic year. Working hours may extend into late afternoon or evening when a school function or meeting is taking place.

Education.   Nursing schools are not the only institutions that need talented instructors. Openings can be found in agencies, schools, hospitals, insurance companies, and health-care corporations. These positions demand clinical experience and at least a BSN. Some institutions require special certification or an advanced degree.

Health-care consultation.   As government and third-party payers become more involved in the delivery of health care, they're seeking experienced nurses to review claims and help with discharge planning. Hospital experience is a must. Familiarity with health legislation, insurance procedures, statistics, and health-care regulations greatly improves a nurse's qualifications. The hours are regular, and the pay may be higher than what nurses earn in a hospital setting.

Product sales. Medical equipment, hospital supply, and pharmaceutical companies often employ nurses to evaluate and sell new products. These companies realize that staff nurses are more apt to buy or recommend products sold by other nurses than by salespeople who have no experience with the products' practical applications. Prospective nurse/ salespeople should have experience in the specialties for which the instruments they are selling are designed. A BSN or a degree in science is often necessary. Salaries are usually better than hospital pay, and commissions can make them even higher. Travel may be required.

Research. A fairly new area for nurses involves research in pharmaceuticals, health-care products, diseases, or human behavior. Someone who is very detail-oriented may be particularly well suited for such a position. Experience in the specialty under study is required, plus a BSN and perhaps even a master's degree or a doctorate. Hours and salaries are usually better than those offered by most hospitals.

Computers. Hardware and software companies need experienced RNs to assist in developing health-care programs and packages. As in almost any nursing discipline, hospital experience is necessary, along with the ability to learn and apply computer technology and some interest in sales and marketing. Salaries tend to be higher than those in hospitals, and the hours are generally regular; some travel may be involved.

Organizational services. More and more organizations are being run by nurses for nurses and the nursing profession. Those interested in professional issues, lobbying, writing, and public speaking may find satisfaction in working for one of these organizations. Clinical experience is usually required, but the need for a degree varies. For the most part, salaries are about the same as those offered by hospitals. Hours tend to be flexible but may involve nights and weekends, as well as some traveling.

Entrepreneurship. Many nurses are starting their own businesses, which range from private nursing practices to consulting firms, from research labs to computer software companies. The only requirements for going into business for yourself are a desire to be autonomous and a willingness to take chances. Entrepreneurs determine their own salaries and hours, of course.

Another growing career possibility, as mentioned earlier, is law. Nurses who are interested in ethics, malpractice, and government regulation, as well as nursing and hospital law, have pursued the Juris Doctor (JD) degree.

For nurses who want to advance their careers while remaining in a hospital situation, the best bet is to become certified in a particular specialty. If your goal is to work as a nurse anesthetist, nurse practitioner, or nurse midwife, you will be required to complete either a master's degree or an accredited certification program. Before you can qualify for certification in many other specialties—critical care, IV therapy, rehabilitation, oncology, and perioperative nursing, for example—you'll need from one to five years of relevant clinical experience.

PHYSICAL THERAPY

For those looking for a career path through the health field that does not lead to becoming a doctor or a nurse, physical therapy holds the promise of a thriving career in the 1990s. On the Department of Labor's list of hot jobs, physical therapy is the third-fastest-growing profession.

Elizabeth M. Fowler of the *New York Times*, explaining about the subject, wrote in the 15 March 1988 issue, "It is easy to pinpoint some reasons. People who live longer suffer more strokes, broken hips, arthritis, and muscular weakness, all of which require long-term therapy. More young and middle-aged people exercise regularly—and such sports as jogging, skiing, and tennis can result in knee and back problems, sprained ankles, and broken bones. Cancer patients and others need therapy after operations to get muscles working."

Physical therapists hold at least a bachelor of science degree with two years of specializing in therapy courses. According to Kenneth D. Davis, director of the department of practice of the American Physical Therapy Association, "The fastest-growing area is private practice, and the hospital-based practice is diminishing. In private practice, physical therapists can earn $50,000 and more. Physical therapists with administrative responsibilities earn $38,000 to more than $45,000. In the Northeast, the average salaried physical therapist earns $33,000, and the non-salaried in private practice earns $70,000."

DENTISTRY

It might seem that entering dentistry these days is flying in the teeth of reality, so to speak. Dental school applications have dropped by about two-thirds since 1975, according to the American Association of Dental Schools, and actual enrollment has been declining since its peak year, 1981 (not coincidentally, the same year that federal grant programs to dental schools were abolished). The slide has been so severe that many dental schools have cut back on class size or resorted to even more stringent remedies: Oral Roberts phased out its dental school in 1985; Emory University's dental school has been transformed into a postdoctoral and research institution; Georgetown University, which once had the largest private dental school in the country, will graduate its last class in the spring of 1990, despite a lawsuit brought by students and faculty in an attempt to block the move.

The decline has largely been attributed to the high cost of dental education and to the diminishing incidence of cavities among children and adults due to fluoridation and better home care, ostensibly resulting in less need for dentists.

Sounds grim for dentists? Listen again. "We have no evidence that demand for dental services is declining," Tony Kiser, secretary of the American Dental Association's Council on Dental Practice, told the *New York Times* in 1987. In fact, the most recent ADA figures show that Americans as a whole spent a record $32.8 billion on dental services in 1987 and that dentists' average income had climbed to some $74,000 as of 1986 and showed no signs of slipping.

So what do these seemingly contradictory pictures add up to? A suitably bright future, in fact. The dwindling enrollments are actually a boon in a field that has been overcrowded in recent years—a reaction in the cycle of supply and demand. In fact, there is a very real possibility of a shortage of dentists several years hence. "Enrollments will continue to decline at least into the middle 1990s," says Eric Solomon, assistant executive director of the American Association of Dental Schools. "I don't like to use words like 'shortage' or 'oversupply'; what happens is that dentists' incomes are affected. We can expect to see strong growth in dental incomes between now and the end of the century— and if enrollments don't bounce back, that growth will be phenomenal." In the *Jobs Rated Almanac* (1988), dentists and orthodontists tied at number 29 out of 250 jobs when rated for outlook for the next few years—and in terms of income they rated 14 and 15.

That income will derive from a variety of options. Our population today includes a smaller proportion of children than it did two or three decades ago, and those children are getting fewer cavities—but there are proportionately more middle-aged and elderly people, with the dental problems of middle and old age. Periodontic (gum) disease remains a major problem. And although cavities can be prevented, crooked teeth and overbites cannot—providing steady work for orthodontists among both young and older patients. Furthermore, as the need for certain types of dentistry declines, the demand for cosmetic and restorative work has been on the rise.

The shape of dental practice is undergoing alterations as well. Traditionally, dental school graduates have either hung out their own shingles or entered a partnership with an established dentist until they could afford to go solo. However, the onerous economic burden imposed today by soaring education costs, expensive high-tech and other equipment, and malpractice insurance is putting pressure on the traditional system. The entire concept of overhead is changing, and that heralds the onset of group practice, according to Dr. Frank Faunce of the Trent Research Institute in Atlanta, Georgia, who is also an ADA spokesman.

"We will have business organizations develop that will not be in the hands of a manager or lawyer, like Humana, but in the hands of the trained practitioners," Faunce predicts. "Management is likely to be one of the most rewarding areas in dentistry in the next few years." Groups are also likely to provide plenty of positions and opportunities for properly trained auxiliary personnel such as dental technicians, hygienists, and assistants, who are also becoming more and more sought-after. (Solomon estimates that in the Washington, DC, area, the number of want ads for dental hygienists has virtually tripled in the last couple of years.)

Facilitating this trend toward consolidation is the continuing development of more sophisticated and expensive equipment. Computers enable the formation of widespread dental group networks—say, with headquarters in Des Moines and offices in rural locations throughout Iowa—which can exchange information at the tap of a key and allow dentists to transmit exact data and images to dental technicians working at another location. Computer imaging systems, still in their infancy in the late eighties, have the potential to add a whole new dimension to cosmetic dentistry—but they are too costly for many individual practitioners.

Another factor, which may have some bearing on cost, is influencing what dentists consider in terms of equipment, says Faunce: the spread of AIDS. Safety procedures are becoming much more strict to prevent cross-contamination: Instruments must be autoclaved, not just cold-sterilized; masks, gloves, and special glasses are becoming standard equipment; even light switches need protective coverings. An action as simple as a dentist writing on a chart and putting his pen back in his pocket can transmit a disease. One solution is an electronic charting system like that developed by Dictaphone—rather more expensive than the old clipboard method.

Changing technology and advances through research, not to mention the possible relative scarcity of dentists by the end of the century, are likely to rescue the hard-pressed field of dental teaching eventually, as well. "If a dentist or doctor knows only what we know today, ten years from now he will be obsolete," declares Faunce. "The emphasis in the health field will change from undergraduate and graduate to postgraduate training, to continuing auxiliary programs sponsored by medical and dental schools. Mothballing facilities and personnel is a terrible waste of money, particularly when we leave so much of the training in the hands of after-dinner speakers. Dental schools haven't taken as much responsibility as they should to train dental assistants and receptionists—and our weakest link is in the smallest positions."

What, then, are some of the promising options for the 1990s?

COSMETIC DENTISTRY

Some describe themselves as "custom smile designers"; others are simply dentists. Whatever the label, what they're practicing is cosmetic dentistry—"they" being, according to the *New York Times,* some 80 percent of the country's more than 130,000 dentists. Cosmetic dentistry can range from creating a special look (fangs or buck teeth) for an actor for a movie role to bleaching to remove discoloration to reconstruction work after an accident—or any of the other work that serves to improve a person's dental appearance.

Very few dentists as yet specialize entirely in cosmetic dentistry—probably fewer than 20, says Dr. Jeff Morley, president of the 500-member American Academy of Cosmetic Dentistry—but for thousands of others it constitutes a substantial part of their practice—generally the fastest-growing and most lucrative part. Dr. Ronald Goldstein, author of *Change Your Smile* and a professor at the Medical College of Georgia, estimated in 1987 that close to half of the dental industry's annual revenues derived from treatment that was at least partially cosmetic. That estimate, suggests Morley, may be a little inflated—but even so, it represents an indication of the phenomenal growth of a discipline that was rare only a decade ago.

A variety of new techniques and materials have given impetus to this upswing: porcelain laminates, veneers that are bonded over existing teeth; composite resin bonding, not as tough but also less expensive; bleaching, to whiten teeth at a relatively low cost. Other innovations, such as ceramic caps and silk bonding techniques, continue to change the aesthetic picture. And on the high-tech horizon are computer imaging systems, which allow a dentist to show the patient on a screen how proposed changes will look when completed. A couple of systems already exist; however, says Morley, "Computer imaging is still not ready. It's too expensive and it doesn't do enough." But, he adds, its time will definitely come.

Just how much in earnings can cosmetic dentistry generate? Says Morley, "By today's standards, the average cosmetic dentist specializing in cosmetic dentistry could earn $100,000 a year."

GERIATRIC DENTISTRY

As our population ages, so do our teeth. But the unusual thing is that, even into old age, they're *our* teeth. "That never used to happen—very few people kept their own teeth beyond age sixty," says Eric Solomon. "Forty or fifty years is a long time for teeth to be around, and they need particular kinds of care." That care runs from standard treatments for cavities and gum disease to cosmetic work, orthodontics for tooth alignment, and other relatively new techniques such as tooth implants.

Sheer numbers, of course, are what will make this particular area of dentistry take off. "Geriatric dentistry is just opening up, we're starting to see just a few training spots for graduates," says Solomon. "We're looking for a lot of growth in the next few years." Training is the same as for dentistry in general, and salaries are likely to be commensurate with those in the field.

DENTAL GROUP MANAGER

As dentists gravitate toward groups, demand will increase rapidly for managers—not just business managers, but investment counselors who also have technical expertise and understand the field from the inside. "I think we're seeing a reversal away from the MBA anything-goes attitude of the sixties and seventies, back to the picture of service to the public," says Faunce. "This opens up a whole new area of specialized management—people who get a medical or dental degree and then go into management. It's a hot new area of learning and will probably develop into specialties in business schools." Some schools, such as Case Western

Reserve, have initiated programs offering concurrent DDS and MBA degrees. Such a dental group manager would also do well to acquire computer expertise to deal with information transfer and the like.

Many dentists who have picked up MBAs, says Solomon, have subsequently set up shop as consultants, offering their services to individual or group practitioners.

DENTAL/MEDICAL LAW

One simple reason explains the need for practitioners experienced in both health and law: malpractice suits, the nemesis of every health-care profession. Malpractice suits and settlements have sent insurance costs soaring. Now, some dentists and physicians are moving to fight back by going to law school and acquiring the expertise to try to fight unnecessary and spurious suits and to change the system. And the system is ripe for change. In the town of Griffin, Georgia, for instance, a grass-roots boycott by health professionals against the family of an attorney who had sued some of them attracted state-wide attention. The incident eventually led to reform of the state's medical system, including guidelines to control nuisance malpractice suits and, subsequently, insurance rates. Such attempts at insurance and regulations reform will provide some intriguing options in the legal arena.

Such dentist-lawyers will be in demand by the same group practices that need group managers. And one step beyond both of these is what Faunce calls "the super management candidate": the dentist or physician who acquires both an MBA *and* law expertise. Such a paragon, he says, would be prime material for top executive positions at pharmaceuticals and health-related companies such as Eli Lilly, Pfizer, and Johnson & Johnson, able to outperform monodimensional executives who are forced to rely on consultants for expertise and advice.

RESEARCH

An increasing amount of money is being poured into dental research, some of it, as in the case of Emory University, as the result of the squeeze in the education field. But researchers are not easy to come by. "Schools and research institutions are really looking for qualified researchers with clinical as well as standard experience," says Solomon. "They're hard to find." Such candidates need at least a master of science, and preferably a PhD, in addition to the dental degree, and will find that salaries are competitive with those in the field of practice.

DENTAL TECHNOLOGY

The dental technology field poses at least one difficulty not found in dentistry as a whole: Because it is not regulated, trained and experienced technicians find themselves in competition with untrained as well as trained practitioners. However, that also means that good, certified technologists are in high demand, especially as demand throughout the industry continues to rise. "In the next ten years, I see a big growth in dentures," says Vincent Alleluia, a board member of the American Society for Master Dental Technologists. "We have saturated the industry with ceramists, but there is a great need for denture technicians—I have ten labs right now who need them, but we simply can't find qualified people."

Qualification in this field is earned by acquiring certification as either a Certified Dental Technologist or a Master Dental Technologist. Salaries for denture technicians, notoriously underpaid in the past, are on the way up with the demand; the manager of a denture technology department at a lab can currently earn $750 to $1,000 a week.

LAW AND PARALEGAL

The legal profession is one of the sure-fire growth industries of the 1990s. No other profession, except perhaps accounting, has seen such a revitalization and increased demand for its expertise and so many clients willing to pay for its "help." Bill Flannagan, senior editor of *Forbes* magazine, says,

> Our present economy couldn't survive without lawyers. The need is for more and more legal services. What with all that wealth flying around, those mega-mergers, buyouts, hostile and friendly takeovers—each deal requires a platoon of lawyers. Someone's got to see about moving all that money around. Without question, Wall Street is the bedrock of the capitalist world, and that foundation is laid for the next hundred years. And with the new tax law, the opportunities for clever lawyers are unlimited. If you think we are up to our necks in lawyers now—just wait. They're going to be like wild animals around a salt lick.

Given the high demand for lawyers in the business sector and the ever more litigious character of our society, it will be hard to strike out in the legal profession in the 1990s. The need for lawyers is clearly reflected in on-campus recruitment by law firms. Jane Thieberger, director of career planning at New York University Law School, notes the increase in entry-level openings and summer internships. Entry-level opportunities for NYC students, reports Thieberger, rose from 460 in 1984 to 855 in 1986—almost double. A survey by the National Association for Law Placement of 1986 law school graduates has found that 61.6 percent entered private practice, almost 10 percentage points higher than in the first such survey in 1974. That rise has been counterweighted by a decrease in new lawyers taking government or public interest jobs. In 1975, for example, 17.6 percent took government jobs; in 1986, 12 percent did. Public interest employment, which peaked at 5.9 percent in 1978, dropped to 3 percent in 1986.

The results of the survey demonstrate how the competitive salaries paid by large law firms are, predictably enough, affecting the legal profession. The average salary at a law firm in 1986 was $36,050, an increase of 13.9 percent from 1985. The figure was up 25 percent in New York City, where Cravath, Swaine & Moore, which generally establishes the top rate there, settled on a salary of $71,077 for 1987 graduates. On the other hand, public interest organizations paid an average starting salary of $21,792 in the same period. And in the federal government, which 20 years ago roughly matched starting salaries at Wall Street firms, a lawyer at a GS-11 rank made $27,172.

The NALP survey indicates that these salaries vary according to size of firm and region of the country. For instance, while at a very small firm (2–10 partners) the mean salary is $24,976, the highest salary can reach $100,000+, as opposed to very large firms, where the mean salary is $48,058 but the highest salary is $73,000. Geography is another differential: The New England states pay the highest salaries and the East South Central states the lowest.

The 31 August 1987 issue of the *National Law Journal* carried a report on a survey of the factors influencing law students' choices of employers with whom they would like to interview on campus. The survey was administered in both 1986 and 1987 before the start of on-campus recruitment at the University of Chicago Law School, Georgetown University Law Center, and New York University School of Law, all of which have large on-campus interviewing programs. It revealed that geographic location was the factor consistently rated "very important" by the highest percentage of students. Of the ten factors influencing choice that were rated "very important" or "moderately important," type of practice placed second after geographical location.

Reputation of employer was third, followed by nice people/ nice atmosphere in fourth, and salary running a close fifth.

Although general practice lawyers are still needed, it is the specialist lawyers who are increasingly in demand. As with medicine, the areas of specialty have shifted according to the changing needs of the country. Fast-track legal careers in the 1990s will depend on expertise not only in law but also in a particular other area as well. The quickest way to a successful practice will be this combination of expertise. Choosing the right specialty and the right law firm are, therefore, important decisions.

The specialty you select should be one in which you have a proclivity and interest, and the firm should be one that not only fits your opportunity, salary, and growth requirements but, more important, includes your specialty in its major areas of practice (see the *Select Guide to Law Firms*, Skeibo press, Mount Vernon, NY).

It should be noted that in most cases, the large top law firms will be prejudiced toward the high-prestige law schools and will be strongly influenced by your standing in the class. If you arrive with a special area of expertise, you will up your chances of being hired.

Let's look at some of the new specialties that are forging ahead.

ENVIRONMENTAL LAW

An article by Robert Reinhold, in the 29 April 1988 *New York Times*, heralds the coming of age of the environmental lawyer. The environmental bar scarcely existed a decade ago, but this legal specialty has grown and matured with startling rapidity. In the firm of Latham & Watkins in Los Angeles, for instance, about 40 of the 450 lawyers in its six offices practice environmental law. David B. Roe, senior attorney for the Environmental Defense Fund in Oakland, California, says, "It has become a standard part of business in a full-service law firm. Firms now advertise that they've got environmental practice."

Why the boom? Demand has been stimulated by the proliferation of environmental laws and regulations in recent years. Environmental considerations have also invaded contract law. Environmental lawyers are routinely consulted on major commercial real estate transactions because buyers and lenders fear inheriting huge cleanup costs from previous toxic dumps or leaks or from asbestos in buildings.

"We are in the middle of an explosion," says Barry C. Groveman, former chief prosecutor for Los Angeles County who now has his own firm specializing in environmental law. "Environmental considerations have profoundly altered business life. Court rulings placing responsibility for environmental malfeasance on top management have put environmental law on the minds of all corporate presidents and managers. Essentially, environmental lawyers help keep clients out of environmental trouble."

Opportunities to develop a strong clientele are manifold. The firm of Sive Paget & Riesel in Manhattan represents such diverse clients as the Sierra Club and the Natural Defense Council, on the one hand, and BFI Industries, disposers of waste, and developer Donald Trump on the other, as well as the city of New York.

From all accounts, the prediction is on the side of a continued boom in environmental law because of renewed attention to air pollution, problems with landfills and garbage disposal, and indoor pollution.

As a specialty, environmental law is particularly complex. According to Daniel E. Selmi, professor of environmental law at Loyola Law School in Los Angeles, "The mental challenge comes as a surprise to some students. They come thinking it's glamorous protecting the environment. Actually, it's very technical, very difficult. There are large doses of science and technical language. It's a hard field to dabble in. Either you practice it or you don't."

Those not intimidated by such a challenge will find plenty of rewards in environmental law—good salaries, an exciting and developing discipline, and a still comparatively unpopulated field.

IMMIGRATION LAW

The *Working Women* magazine issue of July 1987 lists this as one of the 25 hottest careers. The Immigration Reform and Control Act of 1986, initiating sweeping changes in immigration law, has generated a soaring need for lawyers in the area. It has revolutionized hiring practices. Companies are required to keep records on all new employees to prove that foreign workers are authorized to work in the States, and the law mandates stiff penalties for employers who hire undocumented workers. The amount of paperwork, employee turnover, and confusion spawned by the hiring law has prompted scores of companies to hire immigration-law specialists to decode the puzzle.

Immigration specialists will also find a promising crop of clients in the increasing number of foreign companies that are opening offices in the United States. The overwhelming majority of these firms want to staff their U.S. branches with their own nationals. Faced with the complicated and time-consuming chores of securing visas and work permits, they usually engage immigration lawyers to augment the process with a minimum of red tape.

Salaries for lawyers working in these areas of immigration law range from $40,000 to six figures, depending on level of experience and location.

COMPUTER LAW

Computer law is also listed as a hot career by *Working Women* magazine. Lawyers who understand high-tech complexities are in demand in computer and contract law. Court battles over everything from software piracy to computer break-ins are proliferating. The law is in a constant race to keep up with new developments in technology. Another prolific and lucrative area for this cutting-edge specialty is structuring deals and setting policies that will hold up in the high-tech business frontier.

Lawyers who start with computer experience earn $40,000 and can climb to six figures.

ENTERTAINMENT LAW

In the past, the practice of entertainment law, although always glamorous and lucrative, was restricted to a narrow group of clients. Today, with the ascendance of the cult of the personality, entertainment law has broadened to encompass clients ranging from movie and TV stars, rock stars and sports figures to politicians, ex-mistresses, and CEOs turned authors.

"Personalities" now require, along with agents and managers, legal experts who know their way around the business. Performance, hiring, and purchasing contracts have become increasingly complicated, to say nothing of product endorsements and TV appearances. It is not unusual these days for an entertainment lawyer to act as a business manager for his or her clients.

Marc Jacobson, a successful young entertainment attorney in New York, believes it is a field of law that calls for a lawyer who not only knows the field but loves the business and the people.

"It is a very personal practice. You become very close to these clients," he says. There are times you become so enthusiastic about a client's project that you become part of the enterprise. One of the exciting things about being an entertainment lawyer is that you can make deals happen and help create the product. It is a very creative part of law." Many large firms now have entertainment departments.

LEGAL ASSISTANTS/PARALEGALS

According to the Bureau of Labor Statistics, paralegal is the number-one fastest-growing job opportunity for the years 1985–1995. The growth of large law firms is the primary reason behind the demand for paralegals. Paralegals can take over many of the functions once handled by associates. There is a considerable amount of work in a law firm that does not require an attorney. Paralegals do everything from notarizing papers to drafting and negotiating contracts. They have direct client contact and keep corporate records of clients. The only thing they cannot do is give legal advice or make legal decisions. This allows the law firm to free up its associate lawyers to service more clients and generate more income. Paralegals bill their time to clients the same way that lawyers do.

Paralegals are generally required to have a college degree but not a law degree. There are, however, paralegal training courses offered at the Paralegal Training Institute in Philadelphia, as well as at some universities, which award a certificate upon completion. New York University and Adelphi College are considered the most prestigious. The first semester is a general overview including real estate, business, litigation, tax, entertainment, and so on. The second semester is devoted to a specialty of the student's choosing.

Helen Stotler, a 26-year-old paralegal from Indiana, is a graduate of the New York University course. She chose entertainment law as her specialty. It landed her a job in the entertainment division of Carro, Spumbock, Kather and Cuiffo, a large New York City law firm.

"I work for three lawyers and although it is hectic, I love it," she declares. "I am learning all the time. I have more and more responsibility, and more and more client contact." According to Stotler, salaries for paralegals range from $30,000 to $50,000, depending on the employee's qualifications.

"It is an expanding field," Stotler says, "because the demand is great and it allows you many options. You learn so much that you can go anywhere. I know I don't want to be a lawyer, but I am interested in the music field. Someday I may want to go into management, music publishing, or a record company. What I am learning here about the music business is invaluable." Clearly, as Stotler's plans suggest, paralegal skills are very portable—one of the essentials of the 1990s.

Another paralegal, in the same size firm, who switched from working in an investigative firm to doing investigative work in a law firm, is representative of the extensive opportunities offered to paralegals. He prepares cases for trial, gathers information, interviews prospective witnesses, and takes statements and depositions. In the firm he works for now, he primarily prepares libel cases and proxy fights. He says, "Not only is paralegal a booming field, but the possibilities for specialties, dimension, and status are growing. Lawyers are looking for more and more experts as opposed to just clerks. As a paralegal you have to like the law first, and to do what I am doing you need imagination and clever thinking."

He earns more than $70,000, and so do other investigative paralegals.

ENGINEERING

Who will engineer our future? That's a question on the minds of a lot of company executives and industry professionals these days. Like the numbers in the health professions, enrollments in engineering have been dropping since their peak in the early eighties. Yet, according to *Workforce 2000*, a Hudson Institute publication based on Bureau of Labor

Statistics figures, demand for engineers is expected to increase by some 600,000 jobs, or 41 percent, by the year 2000—well above the projected overall 25 percent growth rate in jobs in the economy as a whole. As a result, there is concern (particularly in some highly technical or specialized areas) that the United States, already hard pressed by foreign technological competition from the likes of Germany and Japan, will lose even more ground.

Why the seeming dearth of new talent? Declining numbers of young people, certainly, and also, suggests R.A. Ellis of the Engineering Manpower Commission, some decline in the propensity to choose the field, perhaps because of insufficient math and science training in secondary schools, perhaps because of a perception that engineering is not as promising as it used to be. In the late seventies and early eighties, engineering stole the academic show when it came to career prospects. Salaries for new graduates shot up at phenomenal rates, well over that of inflation, as companies conducted bidding wars to attract needed young staff. That boom has naturally subsided—but that is by no means an indication of a bust. In fact, engineering is currently one of the most aggressively recruited fields on college campuses. "The C students have to do a little scrambling," says Ellis, "but competition among companies for the top graduates is unreal. Some companies try to hook up with top students as early as the sophomore year." Engineers' starting salaries generally still top those of all other new bachelor's degree holders, and the salaries are likely to remain attractive. And so are the opportunities, particularly in some of the newer and more technical subspecialties.

Talking about careers in engineering as a whole is a difficult and almost fruitless task, simply because the profession is so vast. By definition, engineering involves the designing of machinery, products, systems, and processes in order to solve practical technical problems as efficiently and safely as possible. That can mean anything from creating new materials for pacemakers to organizing production systems for Monopoly games to waste management and controlling environmental hazards. It can mean work that is highly theoretical (related to genetic engineering, for instance) or intensely practical (implementing a robotic system on an assembly line).

If any generalization can be made, it is that a large complement of jobs exists—and will always exist—in engineering and that, barring a complete national economic breakdown, they will continue to grow and develop rapidly in the next decades. The rise and fall of "hot" areas of engineering will be affected by various factors, including the economic and political weather (is a field in vogue? is it receiving substantial federal funding?), and new materials and technological advances. Two assets will help engineers track those shifting jobs: transportable skills (which many engineers do indeed have, since most jobs call for cross-disciplinary skills—in, say, mechanical and civil engineering as well as materials), and continuing education to keep up with changes in the field.

New specialties and subspecialties seem to be proliferating at a great rate these days, but underpinning them are still the traditional four big categories of engineering (chemical, civil, electrical, and mechanical), plus two somewhat newer ones (aerospace and industrial), each accounting for significant numbers of the available engineering jobs. Nearly all of them are expected to grow at least as fast as the overall job growth rate, some of them even faster.

Aerospace engineering is the one exception to the faster-than-average growth rule. After a boom during which, linked to federal and especially defense spending, aerospace grew very quickly, the Bureau of Labor Standards predicts a postboom slowdown. It could happen, though, that interest in the space program quickens in response to the current Russian initiative to promote joint explorations and visit

Mars; if that occurs—or if defense spending starts to spiral—aerospace would be infused with new vigor in terms of jobs. Meanwhile, aeronautics and aerospace engineers will find plenty of tasks such as creating new, more efficient, safer planes to replace those in the country's aging commercial air fleets.

Chemical engineering, though still the highest-paying discipline, is expected to show only a moderate growth rate, according to Bureau of Labor Standards projections. This is partly due to a sag in the demand for petroleum engineers, which is likely to continue until oil prices rise and force more domestic activity, partly to anticipated improvements in productivity and contracting out of work. Pharmaceuticals and biochemical engineering, however, offer good prospects.

Civil engineering, the oldest branch of engineering, though it ranks relatively low in pay in the engineering hierarchy and is especially subject to economic swings (which affect construction and federal funding for such things as highways programs), may be looking at an upswing in the next few years. Growth in the population and the economy is likely to spur need for new structures, transportation and water systems, and the like. Not only that, but the nation's infrastructure of highways, reservoirs, airports, and so on, having long been relegated to a back burner when it came to money for improvements, is now crying out for repairs. For instance, the deterioration and in some cases complete collapse of bridges from Connecticut to New York City to Missouri has focused public attention, and presumably funding as well, on this problem. Ellis of the EMC notes that a variety of large civil jobs are currently under way, such as a multi-million-dollar project to completely rebuild and redevelop JFK International Airport in New York.

Electrical and electronic is the heartbeat of a lot of engineering activity, being the profession's largest branch—it accounts for fully a third of all jobs—and is one of the liveliest. The reason, obviously, is the technology boom and the computer/communications revolution, spurred and aided by soaring demand for electrical power. Prospects are excellent, according to the Bureau of Labor Standards, with growth expected to be much faster than average over the next decade due to business and government demand for ever faster and more sophisticated computers and communications systems, consumer demand for appliances and high-tech games, and also perhaps a faculty shortage that will constrict the numbers of new graduates. Although the rewards are high in the electronics field, so is the risk, since high-tech employers tend to come and go quickly as they capitalize on the latest developments. Electrical engineers, however, who work for utilities and power companies, enjoy a very stable, sometimes lifetime, working situation.

Industrial engineering is also expected to enjoy a steady, faster-than-average rise in the 1990s. The emphasis is likely to be on increased productivity and cost-effectiveness of existing organizational and production systems and development of new ones to accommodate new industry and increasingly complex business systems. Industrial engineers may enjoy a good deal of mobility, since their organizational skills are required by every sort of business across the industrial spectrum (not to mention by organizations in such fields as health, on occasion).

Mechanical engineering will benefit both from the growing demand for and complexity of industrial machinery and processes and from drives to develop new energy systems. The latter may indeed become a hot issue as concern over the "greenhouse effect" due to by-products of fossil fuels grows, along with a widespread concern about environmental pollution in general.

Within these major areas, or bridging them, or independently of them, exist numerous specialties—far too numerous and varied to mention all of them here. Some that offer particular promise are described below; most are, not surprisingly, related to recent technological and scientific developments.

The median salary as of early 1988 for engineers as a whole, across all industries and levels of expertise, was $46,050, according to the Engineering Manpower Commission. That figure reflects a growth rate consistently even with or ahead of inflation over several years. Although figures are hard to come by for a specific job title, for which the duties may vary widely and which may pay somewhat less in a government setting, median salary levels by industry as compiled by the EMC are listed in Table 5-1.

BIOENGINEERING

Biotechnology has been making headlines of late, and it has also been making jobs. Several disciplines can be classed under the nomen bioengineering, including biomedical engineering, biochemical engineering, clinical engineering, and even biomechanical engineering, which is more accurately a specialty within biomedical. All of them operate on the cutting edge of science, utilizing new materials and techniques, and sometimes in highly theoretical areas.

Biomedical engineers draw on expertise in such fields as electrical and mechanical engineering to create medical devices such as pacemakers and prosthetic limbs (the specialty of biomechanical engineers), or they may be computer specialists who adapt systems for monitoring patients or handling other situations in a hospital or clinic. Some chemical engineering may be required also, but biochemical engineering is a specialty of its own. Chemical engineering techniques are used to help produce everything from antibiotics to beer, for instance by devising a process to refine or separate a substance that has been created through fermentation. Clinical engineering involves devising and improving health-care delivery systems in hospital and clinical settings.

TABLE 5–1
Median Engineering Salaries by Industry

Aerospace	$42,500
Chemical	$50,700
Construction	$40,050
Consulting/Eng. Services	$46,850
Electrical/Electronic	$43,750
Electric Utilities/Power	$47,250
Machinery	$37,850
Petroleum	$54,100
Research & Development	$52,550

Many factors are fueling the need for bioengineers. New and modified materials are making possible new medical devices and procedures. Intensive research continues on health threats such as cancer and AIDS, which requires unique systems and equipment. The specter of the greenhouse effect and possible future droughts has already spurred work with unusual or new plant strains to provide alternative food supplies—and even work with recombinant DNA, or genetic engineering, can be considered engineering in the strictest sense (that of working with materials and processes for the solution of practical problems); certainly, genetic engineering demands very specialized and carefully designed equipment.

Bioengineering has grown slowly primarily because it presents higher hurdles than many other engineering fields in terms of the knowledge required. Bioengineers need not only a solid engineering background, but also extensive knowledge of the life sciences. A number of graduate-level and doctoral programs have been started, such as an intensive one at Johns Hopkins that awards a joint bioengineering and medical degree. Many bioengineering jobs are in teaching and research or with the government, but more are moving into private industry (pharmaceuticals companies, for instance) or hospitals.

ENVIRONMENTAL ENGINEERING

The government's Superfund sites, public outcries about waste in the oceans, concern over diminishing forests: There's little doubt that the environment is a rallying point in the late 1980s. And for as long as that remains so, environmental engineers will enjoy busy and profitable times. How long *will* that remain so? That's open to question, since environmental issues tend to rise or fall in favor and funding as political administrations change; however, the closer we live together, and the more serious our environmental difficulties, the more stable the field is likely to become. Also, government initiatives that have already been implemented, such as the Clean Air Act and the Water Pollution Act, are not only in place and functioning, but are being periodically updated and strengthened.

Environmental engineers deal with problems of air, water, and land quality control, including hazardous wastes. Some are hired by the government (especially the Environmental Protection Agency, naturally), but a good many work for independent consulting firms or for companies intent on complying with environmental regulations as cost-effectively as possible. Starting salaries in the field, according to an environmental engineer working for ICF Technology, a consulting firm, currently run around $30,000 and can increase quickly.

MANUFACTURING ENGINEERING

Concern over the United States's difficulty in competing with the flood of products pouring off highly efficient production lines abroad has spurred new interest in manufacturing engineering. Greater productivity and efficiency at the factory level in the methods and processes of creating products, with which this field is concerned, is crucial to companies striving to maintain or improve their market positions. As the importance of the field is recognized, more money for training equipment is being funneled into manufacturing engineering programs—and sometimes the equipment itself is being donated, as happened in a move by IBM several years ago.

Few schools actually award a degree in manufacturing engineering, although it is becoming more common. Most engineers still come to the field from chemical, computer, electrical, industrial, or mechanical engineering. One extremely strong emphasis in this field is the use of robotics to streamline production systems, and to this end engineers are assisted by new CAD (computer-assisted design) and CAM (computer-assisted manufacturing) systems.

Manufacturing engineering also often turns out to be a track toward management. Skilled engineers in this field who also obtain an MBA are in even greater demand than those without, and new graduates with this combination can command salaries substantially higher than the already high ones awarded to bachelor's-level workers.

MATERIALS SCIENCE/ENGINEERING

The high-tech revolution that is constantly expanding the limits on what's possible in communications, energy, health, production, transportation, and practically every other aspect of modern life would never have happened without a corresponding revolution in materials. Metals, ceramics, plastics, semiconductors, superconductors, and other materials are the building blocks on which our technology is based. And the need for the careful application of improved materials to perform assorted tasks shows no signs of abating.

The opportunities are myriad. Metal alloys and ceramic materials (which includes all nonmetallic, inorganic materials that require high temperatures for processing) that withstand extreme heat are needed for equipment such as car and jet engines and energy production systems. In the health field, biological ceramics and alloys, which must be nontoxic and durable, are used for everything from filling cavities to creating casings for pacemakers. Pellets of ceramic fuels such as oxides of uranium and plutonium are needed to run the new generation of breeder reactors that are being developed. And semiconductors power the computer industry, while the far-reaching effect of superconductors is just beginning to be felt.

One possible fast track in materials engineering, suggested by Charles Wert in *Opportunities in Materials Science*, is to combine a degree in materials science with a law degree; this can lead to a career handling product liability concerns for companies or for consumer protection agencies.

NUCLEAR ENGINEERING

Despite the bad press nuclear issues receive and the public sentiment against almost anything to do with nuclear power—or perhaps because of these reasons—nuclear engineering offers strong fast-track career possibilities. Although some reactors have been closed or never opened at all, others are and will remain in operation for some time. The total number of job opportunities is expected to grow very little—but the number of graduating nuclear engineers has shrunk by almost half, according to the Department of Energy's Office of Energy Research. "We are facing a shortage in nuclear engineers and health physicists and will continue to do so in the next few years," says senior manpower analyst June Chewning. "And if this trend continues, it could be a serious problem." Also, for a variety of reasons, the average age of the labor force in this field is higher than in engineering as a whole, she reports, and a substantial number of positions will be vacant through retirement. As might be expected, this dearth has caused salaries for nuclear engineers to remain quite high.

This shortage, as Chewning points out, also seriously affects the health field, where nuclear medicine is growing by leaps and bounds, but the number of health physicists has shrunk drastically over the last decade and is only now beginning to recover a little. The amount of training necessary also keeps the numbers low.

Nuclear engineers will also find intriguing opportunities in work with new types of nuclear power, such as breeder reactors and fusion energy. Implementation of a fusion reactor is a long way down the road, according to Chewning, probably in the next century; although not a lot of funding is being given to research right now, that could change with the political climate and energy demands. There are also a variety of peripheral (and sometimes controversial) areas in which nuclear engineering is being applied and tested, such as irradiation of foods as a preservation method.

SOFTWARE ENGINEERING

The reasons for the prominence of this specialty are obvious. And the possibility of a large shortfall of qualified personnel to develop software systems and products used by companies and government in their technical and management structures has prompted an influx of funding in the late 1980s. The Defense Department and federal money, for instance, are behind the Software Engineering Institute at Carnegie-Mellon University in Pittsburgh, whose aim, according to former director Dr. John H. Manley, is to turn software engineering into a recognized discipline and foster the establishment of master's programs.

A software engineer differs from a programmer in scope. He or she certainly needs to know programming and software systems, but also works with accounting, cost management, and business topics to create viable large-scale systems for companies. A successful software engineer will probably combine knowledge of computer science, electrical engineering, and business, and possibly of other fields as well.

SYSTEMS ENGINEERING

Another developing specialty that is coming into its own is systems engineering, which, like many fast-track careers, crosses or blurs the boundaries between disciplines. Until Rensselaer Polytechnic Institute created its Department of Decision Sciences and Engineering Systems in 1986, there were no training programs specifically for systems engineers. The Rensselaer program, masterminded by Dr. Dwight Sangrey, former dean of the engineering school, blends solid basic engineering training with operations research, management of information systems, statistics, cost control, accounting, and advanced mathematics. Graduates will emerge with management as well as computer systems engineering skills, capable of dealing with costs and coordinating a variety of specialties in complex fields such as aerospace engineering.

CHAPTER **6**

Getting the Goods on Sales

"Money is in sales." How often have we heard that bromide? But, in fact, it is a business truth. Selling has always had the built-in potential of a high-paying career. Everything you own, from your car and house to your insurance and stocks, some retailer or salesperson sold to you (or to whoever gave it to you), and in turn someone sold it to the retailer. We are more than ever a consumer nation, a nation of shoppers, purchasers, and acquirers, given to continually updating everything from clothes and cars to stereos and skis—witness the bumper sticker that unashamedly reads "Born to Shop."

Business needs people to sell and promote its products— people who understand the changing marketplace and consumers' needs and preferences. Opportunities for people going into sales in the 1990s will continue to flourish, providing those salespeople keep in touch with new product development, trends, and shopping habits of the customers.

The *Time Magazine* issue of 28 September 1987 featured a look at the Age of McFashion, and noted that nowhere has the marketplace changed more than in retail merchandising, where *convenience* and *casual* are the bywords of the 1990s. Busy, busy baby-boomers, two-income families, and ambitious yuppies are all out there scurrying to earn money. And in most families, this takes two earners. Priorities have shifted from the gourmet cooking-from-scratch days to microwave-oven-fast food. Time for shopping, cooking, and doing the everyday chores is at a premium in today's America. Only the "ladies who lunch" still have the luxury of time to shop.

Specialty store chains that cater to the lifestyle and taste of this new breed of shopper have mushroomed in numbers and sales while the traditional department store giants are either retrenching or closing their doors , altogether. In 1986 the thirty-six Gimbel's stores shut their doors, as did the Ohrbach's chain. Many other department stores are merging or selling regional divisions: Nine of twelve Denver Dry Goods stores closed, and rumor has it that the immense Alexander's store in Manhattan will be the next to go.

Specialty stores have recognized the country's choice for casual, upscale attire that looks good and can be purchased with the same ease as fast food. Conveniently located all over town and offering prepackaged style, specialty stores are ideal for shoppers on the run. Benetton has 700 stores in this country and plans to have 1,000 by 1990. The Limited has 2,857 stores and plans to add another 1,000 by 1990. Walter F. Loeb, a retail analyst at Morgan Stanley, says, "Everywhere you look today, retailers are recognizing the consumers' preference for specialty shopping, whether it's food, apparel, jewelry, or shoes."

Some department stores are streamlining their operations to remain competitive. Bloomingdale's, for example, offers splashy boutiques, and Macy's is planning to open its own specialty shops. Even the established designers such as Ralph Lauren, Liz Claiborne, and WilliWear are opening their own boutiques.

The boom in direct mail and catalog shopping is another indication of the trend toward convenient shortcut shopping. Once reserved for Sears Roebuck and L.L. Bean, catalogs now are a part of product and store merchandising. Catalog sales are soaring, and during Christmas shopping days more than 200 mail-order catalogs crowd the newsstands.

An interesting aside *vis-à-vis* the growing impact of catalogs on the market is the Banana Republic, which started as a catalog business and was so successful that it opened specialty stores. Conversely, stores such as Tiffany's and Saks Fifth Avenue have expanded their marketing into the catalog business.

Although the retail game is fast-paced, volatile, and continually changing, it is clear that for the right people— those who like sales and understand marketing and merchandising—opportunities in sales can be phenomenal.

As in retailing, consumer product companies and industrial manufacturers are incorporating their sales staff into marketing and new product development. Sales representatives are becoming active participants in relaying to their companies what it is consumers want. Automakers and toy companies, steel manufacturers and electronic concerns are bringing their marketing staffs and product designers together to target the market of the people who might buy their products.

Another case in point where sales agents are becoming part of management is in real estate. Real estate chains need smart sales managers to oversee their network of branch offices and are bringing sales agents inside. Sales managers earn salaries as well as bonuses based on their staff's sales.

Those going into sales are advised to choose a company that not only is intent on pleasing the consumer but appreciates the first-hand knowledge of the sales rep. There is no better way into a business than in sales—no better way to learn about a business and no better way to understand about a business. Salespeople are vital to keeping a business afloat. Sales is the one area in which success is "shown." It has been and continues to be a way talent is drawn into a company. A recent study shows that most corporate executives and CEOs came out of sales.

Sales is not for the timid, the tentative, the loner, or the nine-to-fiver. If you are going into sales, whether in retail, insurance, advertising space, or metal casings, you had better be a motivated, ambitious, sociable, smart self-starter. And, since compensation is directly related to effort, a workaholic.

CHAPTER 7

The People Dealers

Some time in the late sixties, people in the work force were redefined as "human resources," and personnel departments were relabeled human resources departments. In 1987, the Bureau of Labor Statistics listed human resources as one of the fields offering the brightest career prospects for the 1990s. The reasons? The shrinking of the labor pool and the slimming down of companies.

Dr. Mary Anne Devanna, research director of Columbia University's Management Institute and director of Executive Education at Columbia's School of Business, believes that, because of the dwindling labor pool, corporate America won't be able to take the work force for granted any more and managers will have to put a higher premium on employees. "Human resources departments will become more powerful in the 1990s," she says. "Succession planning and management development—two areas that human resources executives concentrate on—will become top priorities as companies continue to slim down. They have to get smarter about their bench strength."

The mergering of industrial America has contributed to the demand for human resource directors. Companies laying off thousands of workers at a time need guidance on who should stay, who should go, and how to rehire when business picks up again. A 1987 survey by *Personnel Journal*, a trade publication, identified the top hiring area as Atlanta, a city where the median annual income for high-level human resource executives is $110,000. The other leading cities were Pittsburgh, Washington, DC, Detroit, Chicago, and Dallas/Fort Worth.

Another salient development is the overall business trend toward trimming personnel and streamlining operations. Realizing that they don't need full-time workers for everything, executives have taken to hiring people on a project-to-project basis. These trends have led business to turn to outside specialists in areas once handled by in-house staff—witness the change in personnel management.

EMPLOYEES FOR LEASE

Many companies are phasing out their human resources departments in favor of employee leasing firms, which are proliferating rapidly. Employee leasing companies handle all of the essential personnel services and paperwork, from payroll and health benefits to hiring, firing, and unemployment insurance. Because the leasing agency usually has a larger pool of workers than an individual client company, it enjoys lower costs in health insurance and can pass some of the savings along to its clients. Sy Cohen, president of Employee Leasing of New York, says, "We even determine salary levels, raises, severance pay, and wrongful-termination suits for our clients." In a real sense, the employee works for the leasing agency.

Says Fran Morrissey, president of Staff Management Inc. of Rockland, Illinois, "We're the personnel department for the clients we serve. Small or medium-sized businesses may not have the time or financing to have their own personnel department or extensive medical benefits for employees. So they let the leasing agency take care of that end of the business—and they can spend 100 percent of their time running the company."

Industry insiders predict that the number of leased employees will hit 10 million by 1995. For people trained or experienced in human resources, compensation, or labor law, the opportunities in this thriving field are abundant.

EXECUTIVE STAR SEARCH

A flourishing and highly lucrative career allied to providing personnel is that of executive recruiting. These high-level "headhunters" are sought by corporations to help find top-flight executives. Though most companies are well aware that good people are their most important resource, executives have less time and fewer staff at their disposal to find these candidates themselves. The result: increased demand for recruiters who can spot and win over exceptional talent that will give the client company a competitive edge.

Fed by the feverish changes brought about by mergers and acquisitions, executive recruitment has grown into a multi-million-dollar field with twice as many executive search firms as there were 20 years ago. Although recruiters often specialize in a particular industry or market, general business knowledge is considered the best background. Companies that use recruiters usually pay the equivalent of a third of the candidate's yearly compensation package to the search firm.

One prime specialty within executive recruitment is in computer science experts. Today almost all companies have a computer system, whether they use it to transact business (as in the case of a large brokerage firm] or to keep records and run their own firms.

Norman Scott, a computer science headhunter who works for the A.J. Paul Agency in New York City, says that finding good people is a real problem. "It is impossible to fill the demand for people who have good technical skills as well as interpersonal skills," he says. But the shortage is both challenge and boon to the recruiter. "Because they are in demand, they can draw bigger salaries, and my fee, which is 25 to 30 percent of a year's salary, goes up accordingly," he notes.

Computer science headhunters agree that to do well as a recruiter, you don't actually have to know how to program, design, or analyze a system—but you had better be familiar with everything that's out there in the computer world and keep up with the changes.

Elizabeth M. Fowler noted in her *New York Times* column of 29 November 1988 that in the wake of the wave of management cutbacks and quick takeovers, executive recruiters have also entered the arena of the temporary agency. John W. Noftzger, for instance, gave up his successful ad agency to form the Management Assistance Group in West Hartford, Connecticut, to fill what he saw as "a void in the personnel industry." And management recruiter Ronald J. Diorio has formed a unit of his firm, the Drakewood Company, to provide "interim executive service."

Both agencies find people to fill particular jobs, not a job for a particular person, and receive a fee equal to 20 percent of the placed executive's annual salary from the company. The executive temporary pool consists mainly of middle and top managers who have lost their jobs in cutbacks. The jobs themselves range from closing down or restructuring a bankrupt company to advising on new products to substituting for an ailing executive. The Management Assistance Group, for example, placed a computer marketing executive with a computer company that wanted to reorganize its marketing, while Drakewood provided an investment management company with an acquisitions expert capable of taking a deal from the agreement-in-principle stage to closing. Some specialized firms also handle temporary placements of professionals such as lawyers, accountants, and physicians.

OUTPLACEMENT OPPORTUNITIES

The number of executives and top managers displaced by companies' efforts to make themselves lean, mean, and competitive has increased drastically in recent years. A popular tactic among large companies looking to cut costs is to nudge employees off the payroll by offering tempting early-retirement packages. Then there are those who are fired or laid off in the name of efficiency. All in all, that adds up to an inordinately high number of unemployed, extremely well qualified, midcareer people, many at a loss for what to do. Many of the early retirees are too young to simply stop working, while their counterparts who were let go are battling shock and disorientation.

Enter the so-called outplacement services, a relatively new industry spawned by the downsizing of corporate America. "Outplacement," a euphemism on a par with the unemployed entertainer's "between engagements," is the business of counseling people who have lost their jobs. But there is an innovative twist: It is the corporation, not the former employee, that is the outplacement service's client. The company pays the service a fee (usually 15 percent of the total cash compensation for each individual helped) for assisting its dismissed, laid-off or early retirement employees.

In an article by Rod Willis in *Management Review* (1986), Dr. Adela Oliver, president and founder of Oliver Human Resource Consultants (OHRC), a New York City-based executive outplacement counseling service, says that "virtually all" of the Fortune 1,000 firms are now using such services and that smaller companies are following suit. Dr. Oliver, whose background is in industrial psychology and business, cites a number of benefits, both humane and financial, that accrue from the use of outplacement services.

First, use of such services enhances the company's image with the external world. Also, the company's image as a humane employer can boost internal morale and lessen concerns about future layoffs, as the remaining workers see the company provide severance pay and job-hunting help to their terminated colleagues until they are reemployed. And, says Dr. Oliver, for the company it makes "financial good sense, as well as compassionate good sense." Among the bottom-line benefits she points out are reduced severance pay, because the outplaced person's period of unemployment is usually reduced significantly; fewer lawsuits and accusations of wrongful termination, and therefore fewer out-of- court settlements; reduced unemployment insurance costs; and lower medical claims on company insurance policies. The benefits to the terminated employee, of course, are evident.

Outplacement counseling services range from hand-holding during the initial shock of dismissal to psychological testing, career counseling, and training in job-hunting. Outplacement firms have also become increasingly active in helping people find job leads through both informal networking and computerized job-lead banks.

Career opportunities in outplacement are expanding and, judging by the ongoing spate of mergers and acquisitions, should continue growing in the 1990s. So, what does it take to become a successful outplacement counselor? The Directory of Outplacement Firms suggests:

Excellent counseling skills—a must!

Knowledge of the law in regard to termination, severance packages, and so on.

Familiarity with tests and assessment tools and the ability to interpret such information.

Polished writing skills—essential in developing resumes and letters.

Effective training skills in salesmanship and communications.

Marketing strategy and planning skills.

Knowledge of industries, job functions, and the world of work.

Knowledge of resources—directories, newspapers, associations, search firms, and so on.

Although it is possible to find a position as an outplacement counselor with a BA degree, those with an MA or doctorate in counseling or business will be well ahead when it comes to salary. Ideally, the prospective outplacement counselor should have some work experience in counseling, career planning, tests and measurements, teaching the job search process, management, and business. Someone who doesn't have all, or even most, of the above qualifications need not despair, however; many outplacement firms offer on-the-job training programs for new employees.

IT TAKES TALENT

People "brokering" is big business. Opportunities in the business of managing, selling, and recruiting "talent" are as varied as they are singular. And getting in, whether on one's own or by joining a firm, doesn't require college degrees or extensive training. All it takes is good negotiating skills, an eye for talent, and some savvy about the particular field you're dealing with.

"Talent" no longer refers merely to entertainers. It has become generic: Anyone who as a public figure or performer appears before an audience for a fee or to enhance his or her image is talent, and that includes actors, writers, CEOs, sports figures, artists, musicians, politicians, experts in myriad fields, spokespeople, and assorted "personalities." All these disparate "talents" want someone to bolster their careers and lodge them in the public awareness.

The business of handling people has become more and more specialized, which opens up lots of niches for would-be "handlers." There are sports managers who represent only women tennis players, and literary agents who specialize in thrillers. The public's adulation of the famous has fueled new concepts, as well as increasing the business of existing people-dealers. For instance, the lecture circuit business has mushroomed into a $2 billion-a-year industry. The constant stream of new celebrities from television, far from wrecking the lecture trade as predicted, has instead caused it to boom.

Dan Tyler Moore, director of the International Platform Association, says, "Television has created this tremendous appetite to sit next to all those people you see on the news, on the talk shows, to see them in the flesh." Program bookers for universities, foreign affairs councils, town halls, and women's and men's clubs are willing to pay big fees for the speakers they want.

There are various avenues into the lecture business besides handling the talent directly. For instance, Susan L. Smith worked as a special projects coordinator for Mechanics Hall in Worcester, Massachusetts, a 1,500-seat restored landmark presentation hall. It was her job to create speaker series for the hall, secure the talent, and see to the logistics and arrangements. She was also involved in promoting the hall and acted as a consultant to organizations that booked independent events at the hall, but the largest share of her job was securing and seeing to the talent, and it was the part she liked most.

In an article in the *New York Times* of 31 January 1988 entitled "Celebrity Matchmaker," David Fuller points up this trend. People brokering continues to become more and more finely tuned. The focus of Blackman & Raber, Ltd., is organizing corporate sports promotions and acting as a celebrity broker and consultant to ad agencies and corporations seeking athletes to endorse products. A former agent for sports figures, Marty Blackman shifted from representing talent to providing it to agencies. There is a distinct difference: Not being an agent, Blackman does not have anyone under contract, which means he is not restricted to a list and can look wherever he pleases to find the best person for a client. Corporate executives have also begun to call on Blackman and others like him not only to link them with suitable athletes, but to provide reassurances that those selected carry no hidden bombshells—unsavory secrets or quirks that might tarnish instead of polish the company's image. The trade industry publication *Sports Marketing News* estimates that in 1987, corporations spent some $50 million on endorsements by sports figures—double the amount five years earlier.

Perhaps even more fine-tuned is the New York City-based SpokeSearch, which has carved out a unique area for itself. SpokeSearch specializes in finding not celebrity endorsers, but company spokespeople for products. Television audiences may be most keenly aware of celebrity plugs, but far more subtle and perhaps even more pervasive are the product endorsers who fill a lot of time on local news and talk shows and whose corporate affiliation is not always apparent. Their role is to educate, to be informative and credible.

Ellen Golden, founder of SpokeSearch, had worked for eight years at a large public relations firm, where she became aware of the increasing use of expert spokespeople as endorsers and promoters of products. She was also aware that there were no specialists in spokespersons. "What usually happens when a PR or advertising person gets such an assignment, from my experience," says Golden, "is that they go down to the main Barnes & Noble bookstore, find out who has written a book on the subject, and then try to hire that person."

But that, she decided, was a haphazard way to go about the assignment. A spokesperson, she points out, must be a good ambassador for the product. Her job, as she sees it, is to evaluate the potential spokesperson's expertise and see if she or he would be comfortable with the job while getting the message across. The person must have media presence and appeal and be trained to direct an interview—a crucial point, since interviews, unlike the controlled situations of direct advertising, are ad lib and can take off in sometimes startling directions.

If Kellogg's, for instance, is looking for a physician to talk about the value of oat bran because it is putting a new oat bran cereal on the market, the company needs a respected doctor who truly believes in the nutritional value of oat bran. The doctor's task is to push oat bran without openly pitching Kellogg's new cereal. Or perhaps a hair-care company wants a hair stylist to endorse its new product; the company must be enlightened to the fact that the endorsement must be sincere. Spokespersons, points out Ellen Golden, have their reputations to uphold.

Searching for and casting expert spokespeople has led SpokeSearch into another unusual area—that of lining up expert witnesses for litigation. Law firms need expert witnesses to testify on their clients' behalfs for everything from product liability cases to medical malpractice suits. Once again, the witness must be a credible expert, dignified, confident in his or her knowledge, and with good communication skills. And above all, says Golden, the witness must be able to uncomplicate esoteric information and present it in simple terms so that the jury will understand.

SpokeSearch's success points the way to new opportunities in the dynamics of connecting people. Public relations firms and ad agencies are starting to develop in-house spokesperson specialists, and local markets around the country offer good prospects to other firms like SpokeSearch.

"People who need people," as the song says, "are the luckiest people. . . ." Those in the business of dealing with people in the 1990s—whether it's employee leasing, recruiting, outplacement, or managing talent—might disagree: The people who *serve* those people who need people have an edge when it comes to fast-track careers.

CHAPTER 8

On the Money

"Money is a product," says William Flannagan, senior editor of *Forbes* magazine. "Not only is there more money being moved around the world than at any other time, but the way it is used, packaged, sold, and traded has changed. What used to take a year to access and negotiate a deal, now can be done in two days." The communication explosion has assured that global investing is here to stay. The telecommunications and data processing technology provide an electronic nervous system that can rapidly transact business world-wide. Major financial markets have computer screens up 24 hours a day. It is a business that never sleeps.

The changing picture of finance opens more and more career opportunities for the 1990s. The era of acquisitions, mergers, takeovers, and conglomerates in everything from publishing to banks will, from all evidence, continue in the 1990s. The blizzard of new financial products for consumer investment continues to grow. Despite the market crash of

October 19, 1987, and the devaluation of the dollar, it is generally agreed that Wall Street is the bedrock of the capitalist financial world.

"The foundation has been laid for the next hundred years," William Flannagan says.

The need for innovative credit arrangements, new financing techniques, and understanding of the most profitable use of a company's resources has turned the field of credit into a big business. In recent years, the accounting profession, always a Rock of Gibraltar career, has faced radical but expanding changes involving the needs of clients. The increase in the need for accountants to act as business advisors, instead of only auditors, has upped the demand for accountants and opened new opportunities. All of this change and activity has opened up, shifted old and created new career opportunities in the arena of financial services for the 1990s.

"Of all the areas in finance, a career in Wall Street can be the most lucrative and the most speculative, risky, and volatile." John Westegarde, chairman of Equity Research Associates, is referring to the stock market crash in April 1987.

Before that fateful day of October 19, 1987, the surging financial market had pushed employment in the securities and commodities industry in New York City past 150,000 for the first time, part of a steady growth during the bull market of the last five years, according to the Bureau of Labor Statistics. Within days of the spectacular crash, a Wall Street bloodletting started. In retrenchment, Saloman Inc. and Kidder, Peabody & Co. dismissed 12 to 15 percent of their work force and closed their municipal bond departments. Retail brokers felt the crunch as investors decided to sit and watch before going back into the market. We include this incident more as a warning than as a deterrent for seeking a Wall Street career.

From all indications, the field of investment banking remains positive and strong and should continue to be into the 1990s. Barry Nathanson, president of Richards Consultants, a management recruiting firm, says that there is a strong demand for specialists in mergers and acquisitions at Wall Street firms.

"Mergers and acquisitions remain an important area in investment banking. People experienced in leveraged buyouts and restructuring are particularly valuable." Mr. Nathanson along with others in the field agree that Wall Street firms would be a good place for young people with MBA degrees to gain experience. They estimate, however, that it will take quite a few years for Wall Street to get back to the high earnings of pay-and-bonus levels that relative newcomers earned before the crash of October 19, 1987.

Wall Street today is drastically different than in the early 1970s, when a bear market sent thousands of brokers fleeing. Although many of the retail brokers' registered representatives of New York Stock Exchange member firms left the business after the 1987 crash, the picture was not as bleak as it appeared at first reading. Today there are more products to entice investors back into the market. The public has become more sophisticated financially and by every estimate is awash in cash.

By the winter of 1989 there were clear indications that the individual investor had come back into the market. According to the calculation by the Securities Industry Association, an industry trade group, individual investors have grown more bullish than in the past year and a half since the crash of 1987. Severe market fluctuations notwithstanding, the upturn in the market and retail traders bodes well for stock-brokering to remain a lucrative if somewhat risky career in the 1990s. Although the bull market attracted hordes of new brokers to Wall Street in the middle eighties, there are opportunities for broker-dealers outside of Wall Street. They range from shops with four or five employees selling tax shelters to big outfits, such as Blinder, Robinson, an over-the-counter specialist with 1,800 registered representatives.

Choosing a financial specialty requires acute awareness and expert appraisal of the market. For instance, the largest group targeted for dismissal in the bloodletting on Wall Street in 1987 were municipal bond specialists. The main reason? The Tax Reform Act of 1986 that stripped away the tax-exempt privilege of some types of municipal bond issues, making the tax-free feature of municipals less tantalizing to investors.

In November 1987, a month after the crash, the *New York Times* business section devoted several articles to the future of municipal bonds. Hordes of municipal bond experts were caught off guard. There was jolt after jolt. Saloman Brothers Inc., the industry's titan, shut its municipal finance department; Kidder, Peabody & Co. eliminated more than a third of its muni staff; L. F. Rothchild Inc. and the Continental Illinois National Bank and Trust Company quit the business; E. F. Hutton closed its muni units in five regional offices.

Nicholas Crispi, who heads Crispi Wagner & Company, a management recruiting firm that specializes in the investment area, said that there were few places for these municipal bond people to go. Of course governments have to go on, roads have to be built, and sewers have to go into the ground, so the municipal bond business will not disappear, but it is changing. For those who are interested in specializing in this field, it is essential to know in which way. According to David S. Kidwell, a professor at Tulane University, municipal bond underwriting is becoming a commodity business requiring wide sales networks but not high-priced talent. He maintains that Wall Street firms will cede more of the business to commercial banks.

Many other experts, like Robert Lamb, a professor at New York University's Graduate School of Business Administration, believe the municipal bond slump is temporary.

Professor Lamb says, "I think the industry will come back to $100 billion and will have a ten-year run of at least $100 billion. That's going to be necessary to restore the infrastructure—bridges, tunnels, highways, prisons that are literally just falling apart. That's not to mention toxic waste facilities that are just beginning to be put in."

Donaldson, Lufkin & Jenerette, a subsidiary of Equitable Life Assurance Society of the United States, agrees that the municipal bond business will not go away, and they plan to stay with it. Joseph Harcum and Benedict Marino, managing directors of the firm's muni division, agree that for those who remain in the business the rivalry will be fierce and the work harder. After the Tax Reform Act of 1986, the problem, in short, was that there were too many deal-makers chasing a shrinking number of deals.

Another job opportunity for municipal bond specialists is in the growing number of companies that insure municipal bond underwritings. Jobs with such companies might involve analysis, marketing, and administration. Another alternative is insurance companies, because many are involved in financial planning and management, which includes mutual funds, municipal bonds, and other products.

The financial career area with the greatest potential to remain stable is in mergers and acquisitions. Barry Nathanson of Richards Consultants says, "Even after the 1987 stock market crash, mergers and acquisitions will remain an important area in investment banking."

For those bent on securing Wall Street-type jobs, there remains a demand for securities analysts, for portfolio managers, and for marketing and sales personnel. Leading Wall Street firms' first choice is to hire the best and the brightest. Top companies want people from top schools who were in the top percentile of their class. The coin of the realm foot-in-the-door requirement is an MBA in either finance or economics. If you have not attended one of the favored schools, you may still get a job, but you will probably start in the back office, not up front handling or assisting with a major account. With the globalization of the financial market, a proficiency in several languages can be a real career asset.

BANKING

As the American financial system enters the era of financial conglomerates, banking is following suit. Because of mergers, takeovers, and failures, evidence builds that by the end of the century many of the country's 17,000 banks and savings institutions will have disappeared. The decade of megabanks is on the way. Deregulation of banking and the entry into different parts of the banking business of less-regulated American financial institutions such as brokerage firms and insurance companies have placed banking under intense competitive pressure. The result is likely to be the emergence of a dozen or more huge financial conglomerates with offices throughout the country. These institutions will offer every type of financial service—banking, brokerage, real estate, and insurance. Experts predict that the biggest banks, brokerage firms, and insurance companies will have evolved into financial supermarkets. But not all little banks will disappear. There will always be areas of the country where the big banks will not want to go, as well as specialized products and services that require more personal attention. The consensus is that the biggest concentration will occur on the institutional side of the banking industry, which caters to such large customers as the pension funds that are becoming the dominant investors on Wall Street.

The Supreme Court decision to allow banks to underwrite commercial paper, municipal revenue bonds, and other securities may be the harbinger of the repeal of the Glass-

Steagall Act, which has separated banking from the securities business for more than half a century. If the Act is repealed, big banks will become major players on Wall Street.

Those going into banking will find it essential to get a fix on the changing banking industry. The consolidation may make for fewer available jobs, but the expansion of services offers more opportunity areas. As with leading Wall Street firms, big banks want the best and the brightest from the best schools and an MBA in banking or finance to get you through the door.

FINANCIAL PLANNERS

The deluge of new investment opportunities along with the confusion over tax reform has consumers more and more perplexed about where to invest their money and how to set up their financial lives. Enter the financial planner, up until now a self-described professional who specializes in analyzing individual money situations and suggesting investment strategies. The days of hanging out a shingle and labeling yourself a financial planner are coming to an end. The International Association for Financial Planning and the Institute of Certified Financial Planners have banded together to provide a clearer image of what financial planning is and to establish stricter requirements in the field. Although there are an estimated 250,000 people in the United States who call themselves financial planners, the field is flourishing, and experts agree it should continue as a fast-track career in the 1990s. However, the best way to assure success as a financial planner is to have the proper education and work experience. Elizabeth M. Fowler in her *New York Times* column covered the educational aspect of becoming a financial planner.

The College for Financial Planning in Denver offers a self-study program of six courses followed by examinations, usually done over a period of two years, and awards its graduates a Certified Financial Planner degree. The CFP is now recognized as the principal credential in the field by the International Association for Financial Planning and the Registry of Financial Planning Practitioners, as well as the independent International Board of Standards and Practices for Certified Financial Planners.

Nan S. Mead, communications director for the college, points out that many of the planners are moving from being generalists to specialists to meet the needs of clients who are asking for a particular type of in-depth knowledge, such as retirement planning. To meet this client-driven specialization, the college has developed a master's degree with a new curriculum that includes wealth management, tax planning, estate planning, and retirement planning. The College of Financial Planning is not the only institution in the financial planning field to offer a master's degree. American College, in Bryn Mawr, Pennsylvania, offers students the chance to work for a degree as a chartered financial consultant as well as for a master's degree. Some campus attendance is required, along with home study courses. Many graduates work in the insurance industry. As consumers become more sophisticated, they will look for sanctioned and qualified people to plan their financial futures.

Financial planners are compensated in one of three ways: fee only, commission only, or a combination of both. Most planners use the fee-and-commission approach, charging a relatively small fee for creating the plan and receiving commissions on investment and insurance products bought when the plan is carried out. Financial planners can work for big financial service companies, banks, smaller financial-planning firms, insurance companies, or open their own businesses.

CAREERS IN CREDIT

There are good opportunities in the field of credit. Innovative credit arrangements have become quite usual these days, making the credit area all the more interesting for job seekers. The Credit Research Foundation, which handles continuing education for credit managers, has offered courses on such subjects as Treasury Operations and Profit Strategy, which educates financial executives about new financing techniques, and Planning for Resource Optimization, which stresses the management of working capital. Credit is so big a business that no one knows exactly how many people do this kind of work in America's more than 4 million companies. George N. Christie, executive vice president of the Credit Research Foundation, says the number of credit managers and their assistants runs in the "tens of thousands." Mr. Christie believes education after college is necessary for credit personnel.

"The way a company uses its financial resources has a direct bearing on profitability. It is not enough to rely on inventory control and marketing. No sale is complete until the money is collected, and that is the first obligation of the credit department."

Salaries in credit jobs vary according to qualifications and education. Someone with an MBA in finance and accounting can start at $30,000 while department heads and treasurers of major corporations command six-figure salaries. Career progress for someone in this field might begin at the credit trainee level and move through such positions as credit analyst, senior credit analyst, credit supervisor, credit manager, and director of credit. Above this level would be assistant treasurer or assistant financial vice president. To progress in the credit field, along with having a background in economics, finance, and accounting, it is important to keep attending courses and workshops on new areas and approaches in the credit business. Many universities, such as Dartmouth and Stanford, offer intensive graduate credit summer sessions in credit-related subjects, which include such courses as computer applications to credit, financial decision-making, managerial psychology, international credit and finance, and modern marketing strategy keyed to financial and manufacturing policy.

All of this upscaling and innovation in the field of credit is a clear indication that credit management falls into the category of a fast-track career.

ACCOUNTING

Of all the contenders for fast-track careers in the business of finance, accountants are way up there, if not in the lead. The Department of Labor issued an analysis of job needs for the next decade until the year 2000. It showed that accounting ranked as one of the fastest-growing professions. The Bureau of Statistics estimates that the demand in that field will increase by 40 percent by the year 2000.

"Much faster than average growth in this profession is expected, which should result in favorable opportunities for those with a bachelor's degree or higher degree in accounting," the Bureau said.

Elizabeth M. Fowler devoted a column to the trend in accounting. Kevin Lee, president of Accountancy Personnel, Inc., a job-finding firm in New York City owned by Hays Personnel Services Ltd., says, "There are plenty of openings for young accountants, especially those who are CPAs or who have passed exams for the title of CMA (certified management accountant)." In recent years, the accounting profession has faced radical changes involving the needs of clients. For example, the management consulting and taxation sections of big accounting firms such as Price

Waterhouse are growing faster than the regular auditing area, which has long been the bread-and-butter part of accounting. Companies are looking for more broadly trained accountants. Many clients operate as global businesses, and it is logical for them to expect their accountants to think in global terms.

Francis N. Bonsignore, national director of human resources for Price Waterhouse, says, "We want more liberal arts college graduates who know history and economics, who can communicate well orally and in writing, and have a good knowledge of other cultures. Accountants must look more at the business ramifications of what a client does." To keep up with management consulting, which has become an increasingly competitive business, accountants must become business advisors.

Accountants are no longer tied to working for accounting firms. Along with corporations, big commercial banks, diversified financial concerns such as the American Express Company, and the major Wall Street investment firms have begun to recruit accounting graduates. In a move to compete with such higher-paying employers as investment firms and commercial banks, the major accounting firms have raised the salaries of beginning accountants. They hope by eliminating this pay differential to reverse the exodus of top accounting students to other professions.

Accountants with MBAs in business stand to fare the best. Touch Ross & Company, one of the Big Eight accounting firms, pays $50,000 and more for MBAs.

Since firms now offer more services, accountants have become specialists in taxation, management consulting, and international accounting. The variety of opportunities and demand for accountants promises to increase in the next decade. Source Finance, a recruiting firm, says that in the future accounting jobs are "expected to grow much faster than the average for all occupations, at least through the mid-1990s."

CHAPTER 9

Information, Please

Of all the fast-track careers in the 1990s, none are more promising and more surefire—and changing more rapidly—than those in the information technology industry. Everything from computer design and software development to office automation and telecommunications is pushing the edge of the envelope. The industry's singular focus is on taking a quantum leap into the future, in achieving a new generation of faster, extremely powerful, and yet low-cost computers.

Elizabeth M. Fowler's *New York Times'* careers column covered the impact of these changes. John Diebold, head of the Diebold Group, a management consulting firm specializing in the computer field, believes that further dramatic upheavals of information technology (never the most serene of fields) are under way, which in turn will change the shape of the industry. The continuing rash of corporate mergers and unrelenting pressure on profit margins will tend to eliminate medium-sized companies, because they are neither big enough to do what the giants can nor flexible enough to do what tiny research-oriented firms can.

Experts agree that a critical decision for anyone planning a career in information technology will be whether to join a large company or a small one. Different types of managers will be needed by the two types of companies.

The multi-billion-dollar companies will have the advantages of high-volume output, low-cost manufacturing, quality control, world-wide presence, broad financial resources, and credibility. To encourage creativity, these companies are likely to expand on a strategy that has already proven productive for many of them: setting aside groups of managers in small divisions to work out their own entrepreneurial ideas and giving them bonuses as an incentive.

The successful smaller companies will demand well-developed entrepreneurial skills and an affinity for research, as well as an ability to tap venture capital; they will need highly skilled and motivated technicians. Marvin Cetron, president of Forecasting International, recommends that young managers join the big firms in order to learn their weakest link and then, if they want to be entrepreneurs, go out on their own to provide the service or product to fill that gap.

While the industry's shape is changing, the scope of its work is expected to be greater than ever. Among the expanding areas of computer use are telephony with database services for use in traffic, medical, and security applications and more factory-floor automation, including technology enabling the manufacture of custom-tailored products.

The Bureau of Labor Statistics predicts that in the next decade the number of jobs in manufacturing will decrease sharply and that within manufacturing, the nature of the work will change. There will be more jobs for engineers, managers, computer scientists, and other scientists and for engineering and other technicians. At the same time, there will be fewer jobs for assemblers, laborers, movers, and machine setters. Employment trends through the next decade will mirror manufacturing's need for more sophisticated workers to handle more sophisticated machines. Managers in automated factories are finding that this is a key to superior performance. Workers at these automated plants spend a significant part of their day collecting and sorting data about subjects such as quality control, inventory, and shipments, which are available on television monitors near their machines.

Doran P. Levin, in an article in the *New York Times*, describes this new trend. At the Weyerhauser Company's pulp and paper plant in Longview, Washington, every one of the more than 1,000 workers has access to a television screen and the same data as the plant manager. Knowledge of production data generated by smart machines has enabled workers on the computer-operated sodium hydroxide manufacturing line to save the company millions of dollars in energy costs. Machine operators learned who was using too much water in the process, and corrective measures were taken.

The General Electric Company's Salisbury, North Carolina factory, which makes electrical distribution equipment, is a showcase of worker-driven automation. Because of the phenomenal manufacturing efficiency at Salisbury, GE has been able to close five other plants making the same product while gaining market share on its rivals. And the number of worker-hours per distribution board produced has been reduced by two-thirds. Most important, customer delivery time has been reduced by a factor of ten, and quality has improved. GE wants to replicate what it has accomplished at Salisbury in its world-wide network of more than 300 manufacturing plants.

Ramchandran Jaikumar, a professor at the Harvard Business School, studied the use of flexible machines in the United States and Japan and found that Japanese plants can make about ten times as many products as American factories using similar machines. The Japanese plants, he discovered, also have many more workers with advanced degrees working directly with the machines.

Programmable manufacturing machines are clearly an integral part of the future, as is the need for better-educated and skilled operators of tomorrow's programmable machines.

Gains in productivity and manufacturing efficiency have spurred the widespread use of design automation. This involves the conceptual and logical design, testing, modification, evaluation, manufacturing, and engineering of new products with the aid of a computer. It has become an increasingly useful tool for industries from automotive to architecture, engineering to construction. Design automation companies will continue to benefit from the increasing demand for computer-aided design, computer-aided manufacturing, and computer-aided engineering systems.

Many design-automation companies, pressured by the decline in hardware prices, have shifted toward becoming software suppliers. Integrated Graphics, based in Atlanta, has designed, licenses, and supports an automated system for the $150 billion wood-frame construction industry, enabling home builders to "construct" a house electronically on a computer screen. The system was devised to provide users with flexibility in design, greater accuracy in preconstruction cost projections, and better control over spending for labor and materials. Opportunities in the design automation field should be strong in the 1990s.

The race to supercomputing and artificial intelligence has led to breakthroughs in software programming and hardware design for a new generation of radically different computers. Careerists in the field must be constantly aware of what's new in thought and design in order to remain successful and avoid becoming obsolete.

For instance, engineers are exploring approaches to harnessing many small machines in tandem so that they can attack tasks of increasing magnitude and difficulty. With this approach, known as parallel processing, various parts of a task are assigned to different processing units so that much of the work can be done simultaneously, thus speeding the solution. Major strides have been made toward creating software to control machines based on many processors. Interest in parallel processing is keen among the established computer companies, as well as government agencies. Many experts expect that new parallel machines will soon exceed the performance of some of today's most powerful supercomputers but will cost substantially less.

John Mousourrous, a computer designer and cofounder of the Mips Computer Corporation in Sunnyvale, California, says, "What has happened in the last five years in the computer industry is nothing compared to what is going to happen in the next five."

Another new development in the industry is the plan by IBM and Carnegie-Mellon University to create an experimental, nationwide computer network that will permit high-speed transmission of computer files. The system, the designers believe, has the potential to alter the way office work is done because it will let people use interconnected computers at widely separated sites just as if they were in the same office. The new system, called the Andrew File System, is being designed specifically for a coming generation of high-speed computer networks that will quickly interconnect almost all college campuses and businesses.

The Information Age is in the process of revolutionizing publishing and graphic design as well. Desktop publishing is *the* word in the business of words. The computer has taken over what was once primarily a hands-on business. Software programs can now create page layouts and graphics, allowing the user to place text precisely, reshape pages, and create camera-ready output.

The days of typesetting and mechanicals, to say nothing of drawing boards and T squares, are disappearing from publishing. Many newspapers and magazines have been using electronic composition for some time, and it is widespread in the book industry as well. As costs for both hardware and software have dropped, desktop publishing has become standard procedure at ad agencies, marketing and promotion firms, and direct-mail houses. Thousands of brochures, newsletters, and catalogs are now laid out and designed on desktop computers. Graphic designers are routinely expected to understand and use such equipment and programs and may well have no choice but to become computer-savvy if they want to be successful in publishing. As the industry continues to convert, the existing demand can only increase.

The automating of corporate America has spawned its own share of service opportunities. There are, of course, the ever present consultants who help corporations plan and choose the most efficacious computer systems for their plants. And then there are the computer consultant liaisons, who link their employers—computer manufacturers—to the consultants who help automate corporate America. Consultants play a crucial role in computer sales, so companies are anxious to have them recommend products to their clients. Liaisons try to win over consultants through seminars, newsletters, and conventions. For this field, sophisticated computer know-how combined with a background in sales or marketing is ideal.

Information center managers are the PC gurus of the corporation and will continue to be in demand. Managing training programs, evaluating software, and overseeing equipment installation and minor repair services are all part of the job; so is setting purchasing policies for hardware and software. Information center managers do best in banking, insurance, publishing, and other industries that put a premium on communication and information. They should have a good mix of technical knowledge and managerial skills.

Elizabeth M. Fowler writes about a growing career in the industry. Computer security is a hot topic in this age of viruses and "Trojan horse" programs that can cause havoc in systems—and especially when a company's or even a country's well-being may depend on shielding information from prying eyes. This concern has given rise to a new career, usually titled director of computer security. Most large companies have such managers. Albert H. Decker, partner in charge of information technology security services for the accounting firm of Coopers & Lybrand, says, "You cannot make a computer system 100 percent safe except by turning off the computer." However, there are strategies that help a good deal. His firm offers a service that helps companies to test their systems and establish computer security. Even companies that turn to this outside service usually have in-house positions for security people; one of Decker's clients, a Fortune 500 company, maintains five computer security specialists at its headquarters, plus three at other sites.

Roger O'Connor, a spokesman for Edward Perlin Associates, a compensation consulting firm, says the scramble for computer security has led his company to add the title "computer security executive" to its salary surveys. Many companies, O'Connor notes, tend to go outside to hire such experts, because they don't have time to handle training and they want people with specific systems knowledge. As a result, a lot of computer experts who were working in the back room have landed front-office management positions. Salaries for computer security specialists range from $65,000 to $90,000 a year and can go higher, says O'Connor.

Douglas Tygar, assistant professor in the School of Computer Science at Carnegie-Mellon University in Pittsburgh, says about computer security specialists, "It's a job that just came out of nowhere." He is skeptical about many of the so-called experts and says companies must look carefully for someone of the right background. Computer security managers do not necessarily need an MBA, according to Tygar. "But they do need practical experience and interest in security," he says, as well as solid computer sciences training and, preferably, a familarity with accounting practices.

The computer industry is always pushing new frontiers and opening new career opportunities. Although trends indicate that there is likely to be a glut of computer operators, there will be strong growth in design, engineering, programming, systems analysis, and security. Those who don't want to get thrown by this fast-moving fast track must stay on top of what's happening, get the proper training, and be flexible and ready to change.

CHAPTER 10

Troubleshooters, Inc.

"It's going to be a bumpy decade," announces Martin Greller, president of the management consulting firm Personnel Strategies, Inc., "so fasten your seat belts." That may well be true for a great many of America's companies and corporations, coping with such factors as mergers, takeovers friendly and hostile, intense foreign competition, and shifts in and shrinking of the labor force. But for management consulting firms, these travails can mean a relatively smooth ride.

Time was when companies shunned using outside management consultants or called on them only reluctantly, fearing to make themselves appear unable to cope with their own problems. The majority of consultants then were efficiency experts who primarily reviewed existing operations and suggested ways of making them more productive.

Times have changed. Never has corporate America been in such a state of rapid and extreme flux—and never has the call for the help provided by consultants been louder.

How to yoke together two companies with disparate management systems and decide what changes, who goes? What to eliminate in order to streamline a business, maximizing strengths and market position while sloughing off marginally profitable areas—and how to handle layoffs? How to prepare a successful young company for continuing growth through the tough middle-size stage? These questions have taken on particular urgency as American companies rush to meet the foreign challenge posed by the Japanese and Koreans, not to mention various European companies. Engaging a management consulting firm has come to be viewed as a sign of strength, says one executive at the consulting firm A.T. Kearney—an indication of commitment to growth.

Courted by corporate America, management consulting has grown up into an extremely lucrative and much more complex business. As of 1988, reported James Kennedy, publisher of the industry newsletter *Consultants News*, consulting was a $10 billion business—and still growing at a steady pace. Graduates fresh out of business school are eagerly sought by such top management consulting firms as A.T. Kearney, McKinsey & Company, Arthur D. Little, and Booz, Allan & Hamilton, which offer starting salaries that can reach $50,000. Dozens of smaller concerns are hiring as well. One needn't even have an MBA; even students with BAs can land good positions.

Opportunities beyond the bounds of management consulting firms are proliferating as well; accounting firms, law firms, even client companies themselves have started consulting services. The Washington law firm Arnold & Porter has capitalized on its clients' loyalty and desire to consolidate various services by creating three consulting subsidiaries. The Westinghouse Electric Corporation's IRD Westinghouse branch earns in the neighborhood of $15 million annually by marketing the company's successful productivity and quality improvement programs to the outside world.

Some of the most noticeable growth in consulting affiliates, however, has been at accounting firms, which have been expanding into new areas due to shrinkage of their client lists because of mergers. The Arthur Andersen Management Information Consulting Practice tops the list of management consulting firms with some $1 billion in annual revenues. Consulting is growing quickly at most other large accounting firms. At Coopers & Lybrand, according to Michael Bealmer, national director of systems services consulting, consultants accounted for 21 percent of the company's professionals in 1988, as opposed to 12 percent five years earlier, and the number was continuing to grow.

The services all these consultants perform differ markedly from what those "efficiency experts" used to do. Merely writing reports about what they've observed is no longer nearly enough. "These days a client expects help in everything from strategy to understanding the market to the manufacturing processes to integrating the engineering to the hands-on actual product development," Charles R, LaMantia, chief executive of Arthur D. Little, told the *New York Times*. Implementation is the key word of consulting for the 1990s. Management consulting firms present a plan of action—and then follow up on it to make sure it's working.

San Francisco-based Expansion Technologies, for instance, was called in by a holistic health center in Rhinebeck, New York. The doctors at the Rhinebeck Health Center were concerned about the direction of their business and the administrative problems they were experiencing. After reviewing the center's operations, Expansion Technologies pinpointed what was lacking. In addition, it became evident that some of the center's original goals had already been achieved, and what was needed was a new direction. The consulting company worked with the center to determine a plan of action. That plan was set in motion—but the consulting company didn't bow out; instead, a representative returned every month or so to check on progress and make suggestions for modifying the program, if necessary.

Sometimes management consulting firms help growing or troubled companies reevaluate their directions, working with them on marketing strategy, planning, and meeting revenue goals. At other times, they may help with major restructuring or with organizing training programs to help staff members tackle new situations or tasks as a company changes. And, of course, they have become almost indispensable to companies undergoing mergers, consolidations, and acquisitions.

Personnel Strategies, Inc., the New Jersey-based company operated by Martin Greller, specializes in serving companies about to merge. From his firsthand observation, he anticipates an ongoing need for consultants because of the far-reaching changes taking place in the work world. "Up till now, there has been a surplus of workers, especially for entry-level positions. But in the 1990s, there will be a surplus of middle-management people and a shortage of entry-level people, with nothing in between," says Greller. Dealing with this situation will take some creative solutions on the part of companies and consultants. "Unbundling," moving in-house jobs to outside vendors, will continue to be tricky; companies must respond to such challenges as identifying and keeping people with "company knowledge"—such apparently insignificant information as who's married to whom, which nevertheless plays a vital part in making people feel a part of the company community—and devising more creative systems that reward expertise rather than simply seniority. To accomplish all of these necessary changes, consultants will be more in demand than ever.

The mergering trend is having an effect on the management consulting industry in another way—very directly. As the business of consulting has mushroomed and competition from nontraditional sectors such as accounting and law has intensified, consulting companies themselves have begun moving to acquire their cohorts in an effort

to open out into other specialties. In fact, at least one firm—
O.D. Resources Inc. of Atlanta—has started to make quite
a lucrative business out of counseling other consulting firms
that are going through reorganizations or mergers.

Both specialization and diversity are important in the
consulting field. Smaller firms generally do best by
concentrating on a particular field—insurance, say, or
information technology companies. The larger the firm,
however, the more need for broader offerings to attract more
clients. Some firms funnel money into research facilities such
as science laboratories to bolster their expertise in a particular
area; others buy or merge with small companies that offer
the desired specialty.

Smaller companies, on the other hand, continue to do
well by keeping a relatively narrow focus, by specializing
in one way or another. Market Science Associates, a branch
of Management Science Associates, for example, has found
its niche in marketing management research: The company
doesn't *gather* information, it takes data compiled by other
sources and interprets it to provide a profile of product users
or a segment of the market. The company's selling point?
Impartiality. "We offer an independent, objective interpretation," says Daniel Ray, vice president of Market Science
Associates. "A data gatherer may be biased—there may be
a bias in the way the questions are asked. We try to pinpoint
such problems."

Wherever there's a special market area, there's a potential
niche to be filled by a consultant with the imagination to
see it. One firm, Burdeshaw Associates Ltd. of Bethesda,
Maryland, is an unusual example: The company, whose
founder is a retired Army brigadier general and most of
whose associates are retired admirals and generals from all
branches of the military, advises companies on how to do
business with the Pentagon. To avoid any hint of "old-boy"
networking and running afoul of laws against armed forces

retirees representing commercial interests in dealings with the government, the company does not contract with the government—only with private clients.

Starting a new practice, however, is more and more difficult, as the *New York Times* noted in 1988. The culprits: heavy competition, high costs associated with the need to implement as well as suggest solutions, and the thrust toward expanding internationally.

The global market is luring more and more consulting firms into costly and potentially very lucrative expansions. While domestic consulting firms were showing a growth rate of more than 10 percent a year in the late 1980s, the branches with overseas revenues were swelling by 30 percent annually. American firms have thus far led the way in the world of management consulting, and their greater expertise gives them a distinct advantage in the European nations, Japan, and other countries less practiced in this field; the unifying of the European Economic Community by 1992 offers a particularly rich and challenging arena. But foreign competition in management consulting promises to stiffen as we approach the turn of the century.

Opportunities in small firms and large ones, in international and domestic markets, in fields ranging from health to retail marketing to information science and beyond—clearly, consulting promises lots of fast-track possibilities for the 1990s. And not least among them is the track leading to upper management in some of the client companies themselves, which have been known to make offers to outside consultants who have served them well and gained insight into their workings. Would-be (or working) consultants aiming for the fast track would do well to pick up courses and/or experience in management information systems, computer science, mathematics, engineering, and manufacturing or production, as well as plenty of information relating to whatever specialty they're entering. And then it's on to the fast track

CHAPTER 11

Travel and Leisure

Hospitality management, as it is called in the hotel and restaurant industry, is high up on the government's list of occupations that are expected to grow much faster than average by 1995. This prediction is beyond a promise—it is already taking place.

"Without question, it is a career with wide-open opportunities," says Anthony G. Marshall, dean of the School of Hospitality Management at Florida International University. "We have 100 percent placement success with our graduates."

Says Dr. Fred Antil, director of career planning and placement for Cornell University's School of Hotel Management, "Hotel management is such a positive and expanding field that our people receive on the average three to four job offers upon graduation."

The increase in opportunities is based not solely on the fact that Americans are traveling more and playing more, but also on the broadening conception of and diversity within the industry itself. Today's focus is on what is known as "market segmentation." "The days of the great big 500-room luxury hotels near airports and on the outskirts of cities are over. They have reached their saturation point," says Marshall.

The real growth is in convention hotels, all-suite hotels for business travelers, adult residence hotels for retired persons, and economy-type lodging with fewer amenities. Adult residences and economy-line hotels are particularly significant. All of the major chains—Marriott, Holiday Inn, Howard Johnson, Ramada, even Hilton—are opening smaller 100- to 250-room highway properties and very low priced courtyard motels. They are forgoing large lobbies, fancy dining rooms, and conference rooms for basic lodging. Instead of several dining rooms, there is likely to be a single coffee-shop-type restaurant with cafeteria-style service.

The demand for people to manage all of these facilities far outweighs the supply. Although entry-level pay for, let's say, assistant managers starts in the low to middle twenties, Antil says "there is no ceiling on hospitality salaries." Also, opportunities for promotion are strong. Growing companies are constantly seeking to advance good people within their organizations.

Hotel management includes everything from overseeing housekeeping and the food and beverage operation to understanding the new financial trend of yield management. Airlines have been using yield management for a long time, but it has only recently been applied to the hotel business. It entails knowing at what point to discount rates rather than have empty rooms. Special weekend rates have been offered for some time, but now the concept is spreading to regular daily traffic also.

There are many behind-the-scenes opportunities in marketing, finance, systems analysis, and so on, but essentially hospitality is an up-front, hands-on career. Both Antil and Marshall are adamant that no one should jump into the field without testing it out first. One of the prerequisites for entering both schools is having "sampled" the business on some level, on the premise that only those students who have worked (part-time, summers, or otherwise) in hotels, resorts, restaurants, or nightclubs can know if they are suited to the business. They must enjoy serving people, be willing to work long, hard hours, and appreciate the difference between service and being servile. As Marshall points out, they must also be willing to go against the mainstream. "We work when others sleep. We work when others play," he says. "Their holidays are not ours."

Both schools require good SAT scores and personal interviews in addition to hands-on experience. Cornell is particularly difficult to get into, with only 170 students in the school at a time. It accepts, on average, one out of nine applications; other hopefuls may be put on its waiting list. Although a degree is not absolutely necessary in hospitality management, a field that is admittedly more performance-based than diploma-driven, it can help you get much more than your foot in the door.

Marriott and other hotel chains are building adult residence facilities to cater to a market they consider to be swelling in size and profits. As Marshall sees it, given today's typical nursing homes, corporate America is in this way "funding its own future." Here again hospitality managers will be badly needed.

If hotel management is thriving, food and beverage services are skyrocketing. Despite the high risks any individual restaurant or shop faces in this notoriously labor- and capital-intensive industry, the National Restaurant Association says the food services business is in a boom era. Every category from fast-food and takeout to gourmet fine dining is prospering. The Department of Agriculture estimates that almost half of every dollar Americans spend on food is spent in restaurants. Cheryl Russell says in her book *100 Predictions for the Baby Boom* that baby boomers eat out at least twice a week, on average. Dinner out is now a staple, not a treat. And that translates into continuing demand for managers and chefs for restaurants and hotel kitchens, catering and takeout operations. Says Peter Kump, president of Peter Kump's Cooking School in New York City, "We're seeing tremendous growth in the need for professional cooks. There are openings for about 85,000 chefs every year."

There's more good news for those chefs and managers: The student population has shrunk and, because of demographics, isn't likely to rebound until at least the mid-1990s, according to Robert Nograd, dean of the Culinary School at Johnson and Wales University in Providence, Rhode Island, the largest culinary and hotel university in the country. So again demand far outpaces supply.

Drew Halpern, a graduate of Florida International University's School of Hospitality Management, opted for food management as a career. As a student, he'd worked in restaurants, hotels, nightclubs, and institutions as everything from potwasher to cook to bartender to maitre d'.

"I'm a hands-on-type person. I don't like standing on the sidelines barking orders," he says. "I believe that to be successful in this business, you have to like personalized service, serving the customer."

As a manager of the Miami-based Total Food Service Direction, a contract management firm, he is now responsible for feeding 600 people breakfast and lunch every day in the Citicorp buildings. He handles both purchasing and management.

"My training and experience allow me not to panic if my chef or someone else doesn't show up. I can take over," says Halpern, 27. "Maybe I won't do as well as the chef, but I know how to make a sauce if I have to."

The food service business offers an almost unlimited range of options. Jobs can be found at large hotels, small inns, institutions such as hospitals and universities, airlines, caterers, takeout shops—anyplace where food is served.

Party and convention planners are also in demand. Party planners handle large affairs, small birthday parties, weddings, bar mitzvahs, confirmations, anniversaries, and assorted other events. They may take over part or all the arrangements, including hiring the caterer. Halpern's wife, Laurie, works as a party planner for the Music Association of Miami, a company formed by three local bandleaders to offer one-stop shopping for party services—invitations, floral arrangements, music, entertainment, and so on. In time, Drew and Laurie Halpern hope to combine their training and talents to open their own party catering business.

For people interested in the travel industry, corporate travel is the fast track. While leisure travel is not expected to fall off, corporate travel holds the most promise as a career.

For instance, Harold Seligman is president of Management Alternatives, a travel management consulting firm in Stamford, Connecticut, that advises corporations on how best to handle travel operations. Today, most companies have either an in-house travel management team or an ongoing relationship with an outside agency. Since deregulation has led to widely varying costs corporations look to agents to negotiate for the lowest airfare, as well as other expenses such as hotel and car rental. Since airfare is usually the highest travel expense, it is primarily in this area that companies count on the agent or travel manager.

Those who wish to go into corporate travel management must have knowledge of the industry, usually gained by working for an airline, hotel, or travel agency. The best-qualified travel managers have also studied economics or finance; some travel management people hold MBAs in business finance. Harold Seligman reports good news about salaries for corporate agents or in-house travel managers: They have risen to some $80,000 a year from only $35,000 five years ago.

Another booming segment of the travel industry is the $4 billion meeting and convention market. Ever more corporations, professional associations, and nonprofit groups seem to be gathering for such events as training seminars and sales conferences out of the office and out of town. In the past, arrangements for such events were often handled by an in-house staff member, but increasingly these groups hire pros. Meeting planners take charge of everything, including agenda, transportation, and accommodations.

In our service-oriented age, the ultimate service business remains hospitality and travel management. Travel and leisure hold out excellent fast-track opportunities for the 1990s.

SECTION FOUR

DREAM JOBS: ON YOUR OWN

"Space: the final frontier." We've heard it so often—even those of us who aren't *Star Trek* groupies—that it has come to have the ring of truth. Yet the truth is that there is another frontier much more accessible to most of us that offers plenty of challenge for the modern pioneering spirit: owning one's own business.

Few things are more intrinsic to the contemporary American dream than staking one's own claim, being one's own boss. Every year, thousands of men and women step—or are forced—out of the security of paid jobs and attempt to start their own firms. Many of these companies expire while still in their fledgling state—no one ever said it was easy—but a surprising number succeed. And those that succeed hold out lessons and hope to other would-be pioneers and help perpetuate the cycle of entrepreneurship that drives the economy.

_____

_____

_____

_____

_____

_____

_____

CHAPTER 12

Entrepreneurs Unlimited

You're looking for a challenge, something new and exciting. You're tired of answering to somebody else. You feel your boss doesn't appreciate or act on your best ideas, and you see opportunities being wasted. You think your job is slowly being phased out. There are dozens of reasons and variations of reasons, but they all lead the intrepid to the same conclusion: striking out on their own.

Fortunately, entrepreneurial opportunity, as well as the crusading spirit, is alive and well in America today. According to David Birch in *Job Creation in America*, small start-up firms provided more than 13 million new jobs between 1981 and 1985, while in the same period, the Fortune 500 companies laid off nearly 3 million people. Birch—who is himself an entrepreneur as head of Cognetics, his own business consulting firm—predicts that the need for small and middle-sized businesses will continue through the 1990s. "The large and mega companies are seeking fewer full-time employees and instead are using subcontractors to perform the kinds of tasks that used to be done in-house," he notes. This trend, he concludes, coupled with the growth in the service area, means open-sesame for new businesses.

But starting your own business doesn't automatically mean *succeeding* at your own business. In fact, the vast majority of start-ups fail. Surprisingly, most of the successful entrepreneurs we spoke to agreed that the major stumbling block isn't lack of money—it's having the wrong temperament or the wrong idea. Choosing the start-your-own option, then, requires a careful assessment of your personality, your know-how in the business your choose, and the market.

Clearly, having the right temperament is the first determinant before going it on your own—not everyone can handle the pressures well or happily—and one only you can evaluate. Dr. Leigh McCullough, research director of the Short-Term Psychotherapy Research Project at Beth Israel Medical Center in New York City, cites research that suggests two essential components to the entrepreneurial spirit: "First, a tremendous need for achievement—a drive for success, and a need to show effectiveness. Second, nerve, courage, and confidence." Add to this list willingness to take risks and to work like a demon, and you've got the personality for a successful entrepreneur.

Second, if you choose to open *your own* business, it should be just that. Don't jump into a field that is alien to your interests or expertise. The best bet is to pick an area in which you have had some allied experience. Consider the salad chef who is fired because of an operation cutback and starts catering parties, or the actress who can't find work and becomes an agent, or the PhD in English literature who failed to receive tenure and starts a tutoring service. Not only should you have knowledge of your prospective field, but you should have a genuine liking for it—after all, you'll be living and breathing this business for some time to come.

Third, you must address a real need in the market by filling a gap or carving out a specialty niche. If there are fifteen other shoe companies in town and the market is saturated, your ordinary evening pumps aren't going to sell. But if you have a special idea, a special audience, you're in. Look at what Reebok's aerobics shoes have done for the domestic shoe industry.

Beyond that, it's hard to generalize. The following companies—all young and growing—and their founders all fit this profile, but in other ways they are very different from one another. Our entrepreneurs are found in the fields of science and letters and entertainment, in towns and metropolitan areas and on farms; they come from vastly different backgrounds. But they all share one thing: success.

KEEPING AN EYE ON OPTICS

In 1956, Don Wilson graduated from Lehigh University with a degree in engineering physics and went to work. He did optics-related work for a large company, then tried a small one. Then he ended up back at another large company. But wherever he worked, he was dogged by a growing sense of frustration. It was hard to say which he disliked more— trying to negotiate the minefield of corporate politics or observing the waste of talent and effort all around him. He finished his assigned tasks in less time than expected, only to sit idle. Still, despite his dissatisfaction, it took some time for him to get up the courage to strike out on his own. And when he finally did, it cost him his first marriage, since his wife had very different expectations of their future. But strike out he did, forming a small optics company with two partners in 1965.

Selma Wilson had left college and worked her way through a string of jobs as a singer, a typesetter, a secretary at a New York City magazine, and eventually fetched up as a production manager at a small ad agency. She met

Don when he was in the early stages of his new company and helped him put out his first catalog. After they married, she assisted with advertising and market research and occasionally stepped in to tackle tasks such as bookkeeping when the company was short of employees, gradually becoming familiar with the business.

Then, in 1975, Don was forced out by his partners. Deeply disappointed and strapped for money, he at first saw no alternative to taking another job—but Selma objected. "I knew that in a year or two he'd be right back in this business, so why not do it right away?" she recalls.

Why not, indeed? Today, Optics for Research, the company they started as a basement operation in their home, occupies some 6,500 square feet of space in a building near their house in Caldwell, New Jersey, counts 22 employees, and grosses more than $2 million a year. Its high-tech yet basic products—passive components such as prisms, mirrors, and lenses that are used in areas like laser research—are bought by universities, laser laboratories, communications technology companies, government divisions such as the National Aeronautics and Space Administration and the National Institutes of Health, and corporations ranging from McDonnell Douglas to Walt Disney World.

Their road to success was not without its bumps and curves, however. They had practically no money to start with, except for a loan from a good friend that gave them a little breathing space. "There was a lot of sacrifice and scrimping for a long time. We didn't feel comfortable for about four or five years, when we could finally take more than a 'keep your head above water' wage," says Selma Wilson. "It hurts—you want to do things; both of us had been divorced and we wanted a family. But then Don had to go through that business divorce, too, and we had about ten years of growth to catch up with, because Don's old partners became our competitors and we were in effect selling against ourselves."

But they did have, in addition to a wealth of determination, a client base of Don's contacts from the old company, and they had Don's most important idea: an off-the-shelf approach to optics. Twenty-five years ago, virtually all optics items were custom-made to the client's design. Don Wilson's innovation was to create a catalog line of optics components designed to match up and fit certain sizes of equipment, providing much-needed uniformity and drastically reducing the delivery time. Though Don's first company had already capitalized on this idea, there was still plenty of room left in the optics field when the Wilsons started over.

What they also had was an ideal partnership of the creative and the administrative. While Don worked on design and engineering, Selma handled the business end. In the beginning, she practiced "kitchen economics," fending off unpaid vendors with partial payments to "let them know we hadn't gone down a hole," as she says. "We essentially financed the company on the backs of our vendors. They put up with a lot—but they knew we were good for it, that we had the ability and weren't going to walk out and vanish." Virtually all of Selma's business skills were learned as she went along. "I've never taken any formal courses in accounting or anything like that," she says. "When I need to know something, I get a book about it, sit down, and tough it out." She also made a fortunate choice of consultants in John Tighe, a CPA and systems development specialist who has helped her understand what needs to be done for the company, whether in finance or computing. "It's important to get a good consultant to help you develop systems and programs," says Selma Wilson. "An accountant or lawyer will only give you what you ask for; they won't tell you what to do. *You* have to understand, have to know what you're looking for."

The first Optics for Research catalog was well received, and the second was much larger. Seeing the strong European interest in telecommunications, the Wilsons soon decided to go after the international market; they now have a world-wide network of representatives who help produce abut 25 percent of the company's business. The company has recently moved more into producing devices that mount and use optics components instead of making only the components themselves.

But the core of the company's business remains in components. "We don't want one segment of the business—international, devices, whatever—to dominate," says Selma Wilson. "That would be foolish. Our goal is not to be *so* large, but to find the proper niche markets." Optics for Research prides itself on its flexibility. One of the primary things they sell, say the Wilsons, is their ability to listen to what their customers are saying and then use their expertise to turn those suggestions into reality.

The biggest gratifications of entrepreneuring, according to the Wilsons, are the freedom to explore and to make your own decisions, right or wrong, and to know that you're a major part of helping something to grow. But attaining those gratifications requires grit, independence, and total commitment. Both Wilsons like to be in control, says Selma; fortunately, they found complementary realms to rule within their partnership. They also share a basic vision of the company and its future.

"We have always been conservative and cautious," she says. "This is our living as well as our pleasure. It's a passion with Don and has become a passion with me; doing it right is the only thing that counts."

FOOD FOR TOTS

Baby boomers Martha and David Kimmel have found a successful niche in the current baby boomlet market. Martha, who holds degrees in early childhood development and special education, and David, a graduate of the Culinary Institute of America, combined their individual know-how and primary interests to form Mommy Made (and Daddy too!), a company specializing in preparing, selling, and distributing freshly made-to-order baby food.

Through her work in education, Martha became intrigued with the impact that food allergies and nutrition can have on learning and behavior in children. When the Kimmel's first child was born, Martha decided to prepare her own baby food from fresh ingredients with no salt, sugar, additives, or fillers. And the results (surprise) were very tasty. When friends and neighbors who were also new mothers became interested in learning how to make home-cooked fresh food for their babies, Martha Kimmel started Mommy Made cooking classes in her own home. While Martha's cooking classes were moving from success to success, David was acting as consultant to and generally overseeing the business of the George Lang Restaurant Corporation and had started his own concept-design company for restaurants and hotels.

Martha soon noticed that she was becoming inundated with requests, primarily from working mothers in her classes, for her to fix the Mommy Made foods *for* them. The Kimmels quickly picked up on this as a possible spin-off business. They sent out a questionnaire to some 500 students who had taken Martha's classes, asking if they would buy freshly made baby foods; and if so, would they be willing to pick it up or want it delivered, what price range was acceptable, and so on.

The response was overwhelmingly positive. In analyzing it, the Kimmels found that those interested were primarily well-educated career or professional women in their late twenties to early forties who were economically middle or upper class—and loved the idea of fresh baby food. They realized that they had not only a saleable product, but a ready-made market. So they set out to research the requirements for starting a food company for babies, contacting the Department of Agriculture, the Department of Health, members of the pediatric community, and so on.

The Kimmels decided to use their own money rather than take in outside investors, in order to maintain control of the product and marketing. They took on a pediatrician as a consultant, rented a professional kitchen in Brooklyn, New York, and had it licensed by the Department of Health, then worked up an initial menu and began to test the products over and over for consistency of taste and durability. Mommy Made started with eight fruit and vegetable products and within a year had expanded its menu to twenty-three selections, from meat and poultry purees to toddler foods of pasta dinners and baked apple desserts. In accordance with using only fresh foods, the fruit and vegetable menu changes with the seasons.

In a year's time, Mommy Made (and Daddy too!) increased its distribution to private customers tenfold and was planning to open Mommy Made takeout stores both in and outside the New York metropolitan area. At present, Mommy Made products keep for three days in the refrigerator and for one week in the freezer. In a few years, David Kimmel says, innovations in vacuum packaging will keep the food fresh for three weeks or more, which will in turn revolutionize the baby food market. "Fresh baby food is here to stay," he says. "When fresh food has a longer shelf life, the field will expand to the big boys. We have had some inquiries already," he adds.

Because of the uniqueness of the product and the success of the Kimmels, Mommy Made has received a great deal of media coverage, both locally and nationwide. Bantam Books is publishing *A Mommy Made Cookbook*, for which Martha and David received a generous advance.

Both Kimmels agree that the most important entrepreneurial personality trait is to be willing to stand alone; the second is perseverance. "You have to believe in yourself and not let anyone knock you down," says Martha. "You have to have total commitment, be willing to sacrifice, work all hours, consider no job too demeaning." Adds David, "And when things get tough, don't run to get a job. There was a time when we were down to fourteen dollars in our checking account. We knew we had accounts receivable, so we tried not to panic." Martha admits, however, that she did hustle to get more students for her classes. And both admit that they underestimated their cash flow.

"But we didn't quit," David says firmly. "You have to want to embrace it every day."

MEDICAL LITERACY

Steven Reinberg and Anthony Matturro, both in their late thirties, started Communication Skills in 1985. Their own communication and business skills quickly proved themselves: Just three years later, by the end of 1988, they were billing a million dollars annually.

The two met as coworkers at Educational Directions, Inc. (EDI), a middle-sized company in Westport, Connecticut, that produced educational films for elementary and secondary schools. Before coming to EDI, Reinberg had worked for publisher Prentice Hall's film division in marketing and product development. In researching the market, he'd come across a vacuum: Despite the high number of communities training volunteers and others as emergency medical technicians to man ambulances and emergency vehicles, there appeared to be practically no medical emergency instruction films. So Reinberg approached EDI with the idea of expanding its market into this area. The company liked the idea, and he joined the firm as a vice president serving as medical marketer and product developer of emergency medical films. Among the people he met there was Tony Matturro. Matturro, who had a BBA in accounting and an MBA in financial management, was EDI's company controller; however, he had privately decided early on that he wanted to oversee the financial operations of a business, not merely keep its books.

The two men had limited contact until the owner of EDI decided to move to Akron, Ohio, transferring the major part of EDI's operations with him. Reinberg and Matturro were left to run a skeleton staff of six people in Connecticut. For a year and a half, they did everything from producing product to "picking a paint for the men's room," as Reinberg recalls. And they came to know one another well and realized that they shared a similar view of how to build and run a business. Both knew it was just a matter of time before EDI phased itself out of Westport entirely, and both were adamant about not moving to Ohio. They had opted for the relaxed lifestyle of Westport and had no intention of uprooting their families.

Then, in November 1984, as Reinberg was driving up the Connecticut Thruway to the University of Bridgeport, where he was teaching a course in television scriptwriting and production, he flashed on a fabulous idea. He was so excited that he immediately turned around and went back to Westport to tell Matturro about it, before rushing up to Bridgeport late.

His idea was wonderfully simple: They would themselves become dealers and distributors of educational material by publishing a catalog of educational audiovisuals and books. The catalog would offer the purchaser a wide selection of products all from one source. In addition, the new company would continue to develop, produce, and sell its own product, particularly the medical emergency films and books. It was a natural spin-off and expansion of what they had already been doing at EDI. Not only that, but the business contacts were already in place, and the two would-be partners were trusted, with established reputations as responsible, knowledgable people.

Reinberg and Matturro took the idea to a private investor, who agreed to put up $100,000. By New Year's Day, 1985, they had formed an equal partnership, taken over the lease of their building from EDI, and changed the name over the door to Communication Skills. The two had managed to become entrepreneurs without even changing offices. By almost any standard it was a remarkably smooth transition.

More important, they had created an opportunity and acted on it.

During the next three years, Communication Skills expanded from being a direct marketer of educational material into producing original material for other publishers and producers, then into producing industrial videos for corporate accounts. The company even acted as an ad agency, turning out brochures and newsletters for clients.

While Communication Skills did well the first year, the second year found the partners in a little bit of trouble— but the third year, they were over the top. "The second year was our fault. We tried to force the market. We spent too much money on publicity and advertising. So we cut back on our own salaries and didn't make the same mistake the next year," explains Reinberg. "All businesses are not the same, so you better know your own."

Although the division of responsibility is singularly well-balanced—Reinberg on the creative end, Matturro on the business and financial end—both partners cooperate in doing whatever must be done to get a project out, from proofreading copy to packing and shipping. "We have no shortage of ideas," Reinberg says. "Just of time."

By their own admission, both Reinberg and Matturro are conservative businessmen, and they agree on the personality makeup for a successful entrepreneur. "You have to believe in yourself. Your security has to be in yourself, not in the job. It's a matter of wanting to be captain of your own ship versus wanting the severance package," says Reinberg. "You have to be prepared to do everything yourself, and you have to be thorough. No one will have the same interest as you in the success of your business. If you're going to be a pioneer, know everything you can before going in, and if you're going to compete, do it better or different."

As to staying afloat and making the business a success? Both men are firm in their belief that managing one's own ego is the first priority. "It's the frills, the extras, the conceits, that can overload your company," Reinberg insists. "I don't need someone to bring me coffee, or even to answer the phone for me." He is emphatic about the danger of being overstaffed. "You shouldn't have to create projects for your employees. You're better off hiring people from project to project instead of carrying them on the payroll."

Matturro agrees strongly. "The oversized office and fancy furniture are to impress yourself, not the customer. The customer is impressed by your product and your reliability. Keeping your overhead down is number one." But that doesn't mean avoiding risk altogether. "You have to be willing to take a risk, but not to gamble," Matturro says. The difference? "You don't bet your company. The house wins every time."

BY THE BOOK

Publishing is also the milieu of Rugh Pecan Stolting who had been with Barron's Educational Series, Inc., for sixteen years, the last three as editor-in-chief. "It came time to make a move, and I wanted to do something on my own, to have the flexibility to do the types of things I wanted to do," she says. So she examined her expertise, her contacts, her interests, then found a partner to complement and expand her area of expertise, and started In Plain English, Inc.

The company began as an editorial service for publishers, but Ruth Pecan Stolting was also enamored of the idea of becoming a book producer. "I liked the idea of developing a project and having control over the concept," she says. Her target as a book producer was to generate ideas for trade market books in her area of expertise—namely, guidance and test preparation books. "It was a niche in the field. No one else was doing it," she says. "I had broad experience in dealing with the subject, and my contacts already had confidence in me."

In Plain English, Inc. continued purveying editorial services as a base source of income while moving into book producing. In two years, the company grew dramatically— by over 100 percent. "Nothing frightened me. I think you have to concentrate on your strengths to be successful," Stolting says. She put most of her investment money of $10,000 into equipment—a good computer, a photocopy machine, a typewriter with a memory. "If you've got the right equipment, you can do the work yourself, and even work out of your home," she points out.

Ruth Pecan Stolting enlarged her circle of contacts by getting In Plain English, Inc. listed in the *Literary Market Place*, a massive handbook considered the industry's Bible, and by attending the American Booksellers Association conference.

To go into your own business, Ruth Pecan Stolting says, "you have to be prepared to keep your hands on everything. There is only so much you can delegate. You need endurance. It can be a very uncomfortable situation for a while—long hours, hard work, disappointments. Most important, you must believe in what you are doing and not become discouraged, because just around the bend, it could open up. Most people give up too soon."

AN ELEMENT OF SUCCESS

For most people, radon spells trouble—at best a headache, at worst a disaster, generating health worries and expenses in order to radon-proof homes and other buildings. But for B. V. Alvarez, a racecar driver/owner turned writer, radon spelled opportunity.

In late 1984 and early 1985, radon hit the headlines. After a nuclear power plant worker in Pennsylvania set off a radiation detector, it was discovered that not only his house,

but a startlingly high number of other homes in the East
had accumulated unheard-of concentrations of the naturally
occurring, radioactive gas, which is released by uranium in
rocks and soil. Until then, no one had realized that radon
might be a health hazard. But suddenly, there it was.

And, as it happened, B.V. Alvarez was on the inside track.
Mother Earth News, for which he was working in North
Carolina, had published some articles on the subject, so he
knew more than the average citizen about the problem and
its potential. Moreover, he had some inside news about
Mother Earth News, his employer of about eight years: The
publication was soon to be sold and transferred to New York.
The time was ripe for a move—and, as Alvarez says, "I had
enough cash backed up to get myself into some good trouble."

Other companies, some legitimate, some bogus, had
already jumped at the idea of selling radon-testing devices.
But the field was brand-new, wide open—and incredibly
vast. In fact, the Environmental Protection Agency had
recommended that every house in America be tested, since
the occurrence of radon was not only frequent, as researchers
were discovering, but unpredictable. That added up to more
than 75 million potential customers.

More than 75 million possible customers and fragmented
competition were enough for Alvarez, who had spent most
of his working life as an entrepreneur, on the racing circuit
and elsewhere. He formed Airchek in late 1985 with about
$30,000 of his own savings, solicited advice from his brother
Joseph, a health physicist with the Department of Energy
who'd been involved in such projects as the Three Mile
Island reactor clean-up, and lined up sources for materials
to make the kits and a Texas lab to handle the testing. He
also lined up a partner, Carolyn Sue Amis, whose employer,
a national distributing company, was on the skids. She put
an additional $10,000 into Airchek. By January 1986, Airchek
was selling radon test kits through the mail.

Timeliness was on Airchek's side, and so was the nature
of the business. Radon can only be detected by special

devices, which ensured the company of a market—but the devices themselves are for the most part very simple. Airchek uses one of the two most common varieties, a canister filled with activated charcoal made from cooked ground coconut shells or other suitable materials. When placed in a home or building, the charcoal absorbs radon within a couple of days, after which the canister is sent back to Airchek for testing.

But the very accessibility of the market made it an easy mark for other companies as well, as Alvarez and Amis quickly discovered. By the end of six months, the two were flat broke, their credit cards charged to the limits, their market eroded by a cheaper kit produced by someone with backing from the University of Pittsburgh. They responded by slashing their own prices. By the end of its first year, Airchek made about $500,000. Gross receipts had risen to somewhere close to $2 million by 1988, when the company counted some 40 employees.

Turning the company around has taken a huge investment of time and money as well as creative thinking on the part of the partners, who married in July 1987. "The two of us have probably taken a total of about three days off in three years," says Alvarez. "The nine-to-fivers find it hard to believe that we work seven days a week, sometimes coming in as early as 5 A.M. and not leaving until 8 P.M.— but we do." The vast majority of their profits has been ploughed right back into the company, primarily into its own testing equipment and laboratories (much of it built in-house by Alvarez himself)—and that is paying off handsomely. In its first year, half of Airchek's gross receipts went to the Texas lab that did its testing. Now, Airchek is itself the largest primary radon lab in the country, doing the lab work for other radon testing services, many of which handle radon tests connected with real estate transactions.

This source of business is vital, because the consumer part of the market is very seasonal. "Homeowners generally think of testing only in the winter. Our busiest time is January through March. Then, from April through the early fall, most of our work is for other services," Alvarez notes. Airchek's clients have also included the Department of Energy, various government agencies, entire townships, the State of Connecticut, school systems, hospitals, and dozens of universities.

Having its own equipment also means Airchek can maintain the lowest testing kit price in the industry, which it has done for several years running. Its kits are sold "in every conceivable way," says Alvarez—via mail, at discount stores like K mart, and through special promotions. Airchek gained name recognition through arrangements with *Mother Earth News* and Rodale Press to offer special low rates to subscribers, as well as through promotions through television stations in various parts of the country. Airchek maintains its market with a high reputation, guaranteeing a free replacement kit to customers if there is any problem with or doubt about the results. Airchek also maps radon location data on its computers and provides the information free to the government and media.

Despite Airchek's success, despite the continuing market—radon may build up at any time, so retesting is necessary—the radon business is not an easy one. Many new companies started up in 1988 in the wake of the Environmental Protection Agency's official announcement about the dangers of radon—but most, predicted Alvarez, would be driven out within a year because of the seasonal nature of the market and the cost of lab work. Stricter EPA standards and varying certification procedures from state to state for radon services are also complicating matters.

"A lot of people thought there was easy money to be made, but it's a tough business," says Alvarez. "It's a long, hard life when you're in business for yourself. You can make money, but you sure can't do it if you work five days a week. It's a lifestyle a lot of people love, and a lot won't tolerate."

But for Alvarez, who got used to the "very fast, very hard life" of the racing circuit as a young man, entrepreneuring is a natural. "You have to have guts, be willing to gamble. I'll gamble on myself, my own capabilities—but I won't bet on a football game. I bet on things I have control over."

GOOD, CLEAN FUN

Ray Cassano is an entrepreneur who successfully shifted the nature of his business to fit his own changing beliefs as well as the changing marketplace. In 1974, at age 21, Cassano opened his first nightclub in his hometown of Peoria, Illinois. By 1985, he had six clubs in operation and had been in and out of three others. The clubs were largely discos with DJs or live entertainment and an active bar scene.

Although the clubs were successful, Cassano was growing uncomfortable with what he viewed as the current unsavory nightclub atmosphere. In 1986, he sold his clubs and moved to Clearwater, Florida. There he decided to apply his business expertise to operating drug-free, nonalcoholic discos.

Cassano didn't want to use bank financing because it was both difficult to obtain and very expensive. So he came up with a novel plan of his own. He formed a company, Tone 40 Limited, in which he retained 75 percent ownership, that was the parent organization for a series of clubs called Off Limits. For each club, Cassano rounded up three investors and asked them for loans at the low interest rate of about 5.5 percent. In return for this favorable loan, he gave each of them a 10 percent share in the club forever—and promised to pay them back before any profits from the club were split. The investors put up $150,000, and Tone 40 provided the rest of the money. This helped the company grow very quickly, says Cassano, in comparison to the rate at which the company could have done one club at a time by itself.

Cassano's primary role is to find the investors and establish the club locations. He surveys the areas in which they open and makes sure that the economic growth rate is among the top twenty in the country. Accordingly, Tone 40 had opened two clubs in the Tampa–St. Petersburg area by the end of 1988, and others were under construction in Ramsay, New Jersey; Orange County, California; Sarasota, Florida; Halifax, Nova Scotia; and St. Louis, Missouri. And in 1988, Tone 40 also purchased a building in downtown Clearwater as its headquarters.

"With alcohol consumption on the decline and our superior technology of club building and management, we see expansion continuing at 25 percent a year and profit around 30 percent," Cassano says. Tone 40 has been in the black since the beginning and has used its profits toward expansion.

In addition to the clubs, Cassano saw a merchandising opportunity. He created a line of specially designed Off Limits jewelry and sunglasses, which are sold primarily in the clubs. The sales rate and the response by the clubs' 14- to 21-year-old patrons was so positive that Cassano was able to take those foolproof demographics to trade shows and sell the Off Limits jewelry line to jewelry stores around the country.

As Cassano sees it, the key to successful entrepreneuring is creativity. "You have to want to create something and find as much joy in the creating as in making money. You have to have confidence that you can create something," he says. "Once you have created something—anything—you know you can do it. Take a kid making a sand castle on the beach: Even though the tide comes in and washes it away, he knows he made it once and can do it again. Of course, you have to be willing to work very hard, survey the field, and use your head. You have to know the market. If they want red, you can't give them yellow."

And the reason for Tone 40's success? "Our successful action has been to build better nightclubs than the alcohol ones and offer them to all ages. Added to that is the gratifying bonus that our drug-free and alcohol-free environment has caught the eye of the police, parents, teachers, churches, and other groups. We are successful not only because we know what we are doing, but first because we are a safe place for fun."

RAISING A MIDWESTERN BUSINESS

What do three farm community women do when they are looking for a challenge, something new and exciting to do that will boost their incomes? They form Bordeaux, Inc.— for "bored" and "dough"—and set to work to raise a company worth millions.

In 1980, Bertha Turner and Jean Negley, both teachers, and Julie Lisle, who remodeled houses, decided to venture into business together. Mail order, they thought, was the best idea, allowing them to keep their jobs in their small town of Clarinda, Iowa, and work on the side. So they chose their new company's name, opened a bank account, and chose their first product, a jeweled money clip. They arranged for television advertising in Reno through an agent, bought the clips and jewels and started assembling them, and waited for the orders to pour in. They sold two.

Another idea was in order. Then Bertha Turner returned from a trip with an appliqued sweatshirt from a craft show. "We could do this!" she told the others. And they did.

This time, the three entrepreneurs started closer to home, appliqueing sweatshirts and selling them to schoolchildren in the area. The shirts proved immensely popular, selling as fast as they could turn them out. If Clarinda people enjoyed their product so much, the women reasoned, why wouldn't other people feel the same way? So on January 1, 1981, Bordeaux went wholesale and started into an extended period of growth.

Bordeaux, which started with an investment of about $2,500 by each of the three, was soon prospering so much that the three founders quit their other jobs and began to hire other local women to applique trimmings on the garments. The company concentrated at first on jogging suits, then gradually expanded into doing applique on other leisurewear. Bordeaux opened a store locally, then another nearby, and began expanding its retail chain. Within six years, it had become one of the largest employers in the economically depressed Midwest, with a network of some 150 seamstresses working in their homes in communities in both Iowa and Missouri. The company's annual gross sales registered at about $3 million.

But in 1987, they ran into trouble—with the government. There are legal restrictions on hiring employees to work on some types of garments in their own homes, and Bordeaux was sued by the Department of Labor for allegedly running afoul of these regulations. Bordeaux fought, protesting that the women were independent contractors, not employees. A settlement, whose terms remained confidential at the request of the Labor Department, was finally reached in 1988.

Whatever the settlement and wherever right might lie in the case, the effects on Bordeaux were deeply felt. Cracks began to show in the partnership, and Bertha Turner left in 1987. Revenues dropped, both because of the suit and because sales had been soft. But the other two partners carried on, modifying their business tactics and relying on management professionals to help them cope with both business demands and government policy. They dissolved their old home network, instead opening a manufacturing facility in nearby Bedford, Iowa. As of late 1988, it and their headquarters/retail outlet in Clarinda employed only about 25 people. Bordeaux also counted about 30 other employees in its retail stores in Kansas City, St. Louis, Miami, and New Orleans and planned to open two more stores within the next year or two, ready to tackle the future with renewed vigor.

Cofounder Negley attributes Bordeaux's success largely to the partnership that gave rise to it. "It's easier with three people. Each of us brought different qualities to the business, and our three husbands contributed different assistance, too—my husband is an engineer, a technician, Julie's is the head of a manufacturing firm, and Bertha's is an attorney.

Like many other entrepreneurs, Negley emphasizes determination, willingness to work, and stamina as necessary qualities of entrepreneuring. "Business *is* problems; it's how you solve them that makes it interesting. There's a real satisfaction in accomplishing what you set out to do. And don't be afraid to ask for counsel, advice," she urges. "There are lots of people out there who can help. And if they've been through it, they may be able to help you steer clear of a mistake or problem."

THE SPA LIFE

In 1980, Noel De Caprio, a hairdresser by training, was part owner of a fairly successful beauty salon in Stamford, Connecticut. But before the year was out, one of her partners had died and the other, a colorist, decided to pull up stakes and depart—taking the customer files with him. This left De Caprio the sole owner of the shop, but minus the colorist's important clientele file, which was the key to a major part of the shop's income.

A disciple of the Lee Iacocca school of success, De Caprio made up her mind not to get mad, but to get even. Instead of pulling back, she decided to expand beyond being just a cut, shampoo, set, and manicure shop.

Noel, a spa enthusiast, had spent most of her vacation time visiting spas around the world and was aware of the phenomenal success of health and beauty spas that were concerned with the maintenance and rejuvenation of the body as well as with cosmetic beauty. She ascertained that there was a sizable market of people who would like to get away on a spa vacation, who had the money but not the time. So she decided she would incorporate the answers to the needs of that group into her salon. It would include everything from various types of facials, body wraps, massage therapy, steam showers, and aerobics to haircuts and manicures. It would be a day spa, combining beauty salon and spa services under one roof, where clients could choose one service, or a full spa day, or anything between.

De Caprio was convinced that the market existed and knew there was no one in the area doing anything like what she envisioned. But convincing her bank was another matter. Armed with facts, figures, and demographics, she went to the local bank where she'd had her accounts for years and asked for a loan of $40,000. They turned her down. She believes the rejection was based on the bias that a woman in business on her own constituted an especially high financial risk. Undaunted, she approached an "underdog" bank, one that was looking for business; it agreed to the loan.

With the bank loan and an additional $10,000 her mother contributed from her hard-earned savings as a cleaning woman, De Caprio took over another 1,500 square feet of space upstairs from her shop, doubling the salon's size, and began to remodel the salon into a spa. Given her past experience, she did not want any partners or outside investors to interfere with the financial or quality control of her business. She renamed her place Noelle: The Day Spa, hired a carefully selected staff of eight people, and opened her door.

Noel De Caprio had a clear idea of how she wanted to run her business, an image of how it should look, and a true sense of its ambience. She knew that service and results were the key to the Day Spa's success. It was essential both to continually attract new clients and to build a continuing relationship with old clients. Marketing and advertising, as well as word of mouth, drew the new clients, and the spa's focus on personal comfort and satisfaction kept them coming back. She also knew that her business rested in her staff's hands. So she insisted that everyone on the staff look, act, and be professional. She chose a manager for each department, instituted monthly staff meetings and an employee-of-the-month program, and bestowed bonuses and all manner of other incentives.

By 1988, her staff had swelled from the original eight to forty-six, and about two hundred people, on average, were availing themselves of Noelle: The Day Spa services every day, six days a week. And the business was grossing $2 million a year.

Noelle's success had not gone unnoticed. Three years earlier, in 1985, the Gillette Corporation was looking to get into the beauty/spa business. They sent two executives, unannounced, to the Day Spa for two of Noelle's Day of Beauty treatments. The execs were so impressed that Gillette offered De Caprio a lucrative three-year contract giving them the right to open day spas around the country under the Noelle name.

De Caprio knew she needed a high-powered lawyer and was fortunate to find one who was "a deal maker, not a deal breaker." He was kept busy. A year later, Gillette was poised to expand into the cosmetic and skin care field. Their chemists worked with Noel to develop a complete line of products, which were marketed under the Noelle name and logo. And by 1988, Gillette had offered to buy out Noelle: The Day Spa, and have De Caprio continue to run the business.

It was an attractive deal—but Noel De Caprio said no. There was something more than money involved for her. "I love my business too much," she admits. But her association with Gillette paid off in other ways—by teaching her the importance of retailing, for instance. Applying the lessons she learned at Gillette, De Caprio started a marketing campaign to sell spa gift certificates and to sell the cosmetic and skin products on her own. Today, the gift certificates account for close to $90,000 a year in sales, and De Caprio is beginning to distribute the Noelle products in stores.

The business continues to expand in size and services. The spa has acquired another 3,000 square feet of space and added hydrotherapy treatments, Swiss showers, and special services and facilities just for men.

One of the reasons for her success, Noel De Caprio believes, is that she is good to her people. She singles out productive employees for rewards such as cars and trips to Paris. Another reason is her total involvement. "I am always on the scene to control quality," she says.

"To be successful as an entrepreneur, you can't be lazy, and you can't be sick. You have to set an example and go to work every day. To be in a service business like mine, you have to have a knack for handling people and surround yourself with a staff that respects excellence."

She concludes, "You must be goal-oriented but never satisfied; most of all, be secure in yourself. It goes without saying that you should love what you're doing and want more than anything else to succeed."

CHAPTER 13

Reprise

By the 1990s, American society will be dominated by the middle-aged. The baby boomers, the all-time biggest consumer market in history, will have moved from young and yuppie to middle-aged and middle-class. In the nineties, they will hit their peak earning years and will, therefore, be the most affluent group as well. The older and richer the boomers become, the stronger their economic clout. Careers that cater to their needs, interests, and indulgences are earmarked for success.

"Cater" is the operative word for this generation that has grown up to Service America. In the past decades, we have been involved in a transformation from manufacturing to services, and by 1995, a startling 71 percent of all American workers will pick up their paychecks at white-collar or service jobs. For fast-track, high reward jobs, service opportunities run away with the prize.

What makes one person's career take off and another's head for a dead end? It is seldom a matter of the career itself but of knowing how to angle into it. The most important factor in shaping a successful fast-track career in the nineties will be commitment of attention to the forces of influence and to changes and trends in the job market and marketplace.

It is crucial to find out whether you have the temperament for a fast-track career. Dr. Francis X. Clifton, a psychotherapist and director of the Center for International Living, believes it requires two essential traits: an intense "willingness" coupled with active intelligence, and an internal sense of time that is directed toward the present. Fast-trackers, in other words, are those driven to give form to their plans and who look to the future rather than the past for solutions.

TRACKING THE FAST TRACK

The traditional professions are changing direction to meet the needs of our changing population and adapt to our evolving economy and technology. The two most significant trends here are the development of niche specialties and the combining of two professions into one fast-track career.

In medicine, some of the most promising specialties will be geriatrics, sports medicine, rehabilitation, preventive medicine, oncology, emergency medicine, and AIDS. Psychiatrists will be needed to help cope with drug and alcohol abuse.

Nurses also are specializing in everything from oncology to geriatrics and finding nonhospital options such as health-care consulting, medical product sales, and pharmaceutical research. Those interested in ethics, malpractice, and government regulation will also encounter growing demand for nurses who also have legal expertise.

With the aging of our population, physical therapy will be ever more important. People who live longer suffer more strokes, broken hips, arthritis, and muscular weakness, all of which require long-term therapy.

The diminishing incidence of cavities among children and adults is pushing dentists into new specialties. Cosmetic and reconstructive dentistry, orthodontistry, and geriatric dentistry offer challenging possibilities. Some practitioners also predict movement of dentists into group practices, which will need managers—not just business managers, but business managers who also are dentists and understand the field from within.

Given the high demand for lawyers in the business sector and the ever more litigious character of our society, it will be hard to strike out in the legal profession in the 1990s. As in other fields, the specialist will be the hottest property. The new tax law has created unlimited opportunities for good tax lawyers, and mega-mergers, buyouts, and takeovers will keep corporate lawyers hopping. Other rising stars are environmental law, immigration law, computer law, and entertainment law. Paralegals are also at a premium to support the demand for legal services: the BLS cites paralegal as the fastest-growing job opportunity for the years 1985 to 1995.

In engineering, boundaries between specialties are blurring and subspecialties are developing. Among those engineering fields expected to enjoy a faster-than-average rise in the 1990s are electrical and electronic engineering, industrial engineering, mechanical engineering, bioengineering, environmental engineering, materials science engineering, and software and systems engineering.

Accompanying the changes in the tax laws and deregulation is a boom in the financial services sector. Never before has there been such demand for financial planning and consulting services, as well as investment counseling.

The services of people and the service of dealing with people are increasingly valuable commodities. In the process of streamlining and specializing, businesses increasingly entrust the details of personnel management to outside specialists. Staff contracting firms are thriving, as are executive search firms, headhunters, and managers of talent in the entertainment, arts, and sports worlds.

We are now more than ever a nation of consumers, but the business of retailing is undergoing a dramatic change. Catalog sales are soaring, and in many industries the death of the traditional salesperson has been accompanied by the rise of a new breed: the field representative. Many department stores have been transformed into specialty stores, gathering separately managed manufacturers' boutiques under one roof. As in retailing, consumer product companies and industrial manufacturers are incorporating their sales staff into marketing and new product development. In real estate, sales agents are becoming part of management.

The Information Age is upon us; the information technology industry continues to change the way we communicate and do business. Fast-track careers and new opportunities abound. Everything from computer design to software design to office automation to telecommunications is pushing the edge of the envelope. With the advent of desktop publishing, even graphic designers must adapt to the new computer equipment. The major opportunities in the information industry will be in design, engineering, programming, systems analysis, and security.

In keeping with the trend toward using outside consultants, companies are relying on convention and conference planners and designers of sales presentations for services once provided in-house. Qualified hotel and restaurant administrators as well as chefs are in high demand because of our population's mobility and preference for the good life, including traveling and dining out.

Although companies once hated to bring in outside "efficiency experts," fearing to appear unable to handle their own problems, today management consultants are seen as indispensable. Their role has expanded to include everything from evaluating salary practices and corporate structure to conducting psychological testing of candidates for important positions and industry-wide surveys of competitors.

ENTREPRENEURING

Entrepreneuring, though it encompasses many of the areas already discussed, is in a class by itself. The majority of jobs in America are created by small start-up or expanding companies, and the current trends toward streamlining, specialization, and deregulation are conducive to entrepreneuring. The most successful new companies are those that come up with a new idea or modify an old one to fill a niche need. To move your idea to success requires singleness of purpose, hard work, long hours, and a strong belief in yourself.

A successful career is a mix of opportunity, financial reward, and personal affinity. It should be something you enjoy doing, or you won't do it well. We wish you luck in connecting with the fast-track career of your choice.

INDEX